The Destruction of Young Lawyers: Beyond One L

D1086215

The Destruction of Young Lawyers:

Beyond One L

Douglas Litowitz

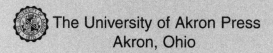 The University of Akron Press
Akron, Ohio

All inquiries and permissions requests should be addressed to the publisher,
The University of Akron Press, Akron, OH 44325-1703
Manufactured in the United States of America
First edition 2006
09 08 07 06 05 5 4 3 2 1
Library of Congress Cataloging-in-Publication Data
Litowitz, Douglas E.
  The Destruction of Young Lawyers : Beyond One L / Douglas Litowitz.–
1st ed.
      p. cm. — (Series on law, politics, and society)
  Includes bibliographical references and index.
  ISBN 1-931968-26-8 (hardcover: alk. paper)
  ISBN 1-931968-31-4 (paperback: alk. paper)
  1. Lawyers—United States—Psychology. 2. Practice of law—United
States—Psychological aspects. I. Title. II. Series.
KF298.L58 2005
340'.023'73--dc22
                                                              2004030053
The paper used in this publication meets the minimum requirements of
American National Standard for Information Sciences—Permanence of
Paper for Printed Library Materials, ANSI Z39.48—1984. ∞

Contents

Anyone who wishes to understand the legal crises that envelop the contemporary scene—in the cities, in the environment, in the courts, in the marketplace, in public services, in the corporate-government arenas and in Washington—should come to grips with the legal flow chart that begins with the law schools and ends with the law firms, particularly the large corporate law firms.

—Ralph Nader, in the *New Republic*

chapter one:
Unhappy Young Lawyers

Lawyers are pathologically unhappy. The problem reached public consciousness about fifteen years ago with initial warnings that lawyers were experiencing mental health problems and "running from the law."[1] In 1991, the American Bar Association acknowledged that the legal profession was at the "breaking point" due to an "emerging crisis in the quality of lawyers' health and lives."[2] By 1995, the chair of the ABA's Committee on Professionalism admitted that lawyers were leaving the profession because it had become "a nasty business" and was "no longer fun."[3] By the mid-1990s, the *Wall Street Journal* was consulting psychoanalysts to figure out why lawyers had become "depressed, anxious, bored insomniacs,"[4] and newspapers on both coasts were reporting that lawyers were "miserable with the legal life."[5] Books with ominous titles such as *The Betrayed Profession, Law versus Life*, and *The Lost Lawyer* started to appear.[6] Even Justice Sandra Day O'Connor of the United States Supreme Court proclaimed that lawyers were becoming "a profoundly unhappy lot," and that they were "dissatisfied with their professional lives."[7] When she attended the thirtieth anniversary of her Stanford law school class, she was shocked that the vast majority of alumni responded to a questionnaire by saying that they would not enter the profession if given another chance.[8] And fellow Supreme Court justice Stephen Breyer noted that "lawyers increasingly describe their profession in negative terms" and have a "negative contemporary image" as hostile, narrow, and detached.[9]

These gloomy assessments come from the *mainstream* of the legal profession, not from an underground band of disgruntled outcasts. And the bad news is buttressed by a mountain of empirical data. It is now well established that public perception of lawyers is at an all-time low;[10] lawyers are reporting record levels of dissatisfaction, substance abuse, and mental illness;[11] one-third of attorneys appear to be clinically depressed, alcoholic, or addicted to drugs;[12] and attorneys are reporting anxiety levels at least double (and perhaps up to five times greater than) those of the general population.[13] For the first time in recent memory, a cottage industry has sprung up to help lawyers find ways to leave the profession,[14] and indeed a recent survey by the *New York Law Journal* found that 40 percent of young associates at large firms plan to leave the profession.[15] All of the available evidence—anecdotal and statistical—points to the inescapable conclusion that the legal profession makes young people unhappy, anxious, depressed, and desperate.

The problem is particularly acute for young lawyers, who shoulder most of the misery within the profession. Unlike their older counterparts, young lawyers cannot reminisce about the good old days when lawyers were "civil" and "professional." In fact, young lawyers are morosely unhappy and pessimistic, often buried under a mountain of debt, and scraping to get jobs that offer very little long-term security yet require immense personal sacrifice. No matter how much complaining we hear from older lawyers, there is no question that younger lawyers have it worse.

Law is no longer a safe profession, either economically or psychologically, and the trouble starts very early, in the first days of law school. As we will see, most lawyers hate law school with a passion, for good reason, but they pay dearly for the experience. Law student debt now *averages* $80,000 per student, the bulk of which consists of law school tuition, which has quadrupled in the last two decades.[16] It is true that starting salaries for graduates of elite law schools can go up to $150,000, but the sad truth is that the median income of a law school graduate is presently below $60,000 and the path upward is slow and winding.[17] That salary does not go very far in Chicago or Los Angeles (let alone in cities where housing costs are exorbitant, like New York or San Francisco), especially when carrying a massive debt load.[18] When a recent graduate of Stanford Law School turned to prostitution to repay some of her $300,000 debt, the dominant feeling among fellow students was not outrage but empathy.[19]

Although prior generations of young lawyers carried *some* debt, the amount is insignificant compared to the debt carried by recent law school graduates. And unlike recent graduates, prior generations could often bank on a decent-paying job upon graduation. In those days, even if a job with an established firm was not forthcoming, it was not unusual for a recent graduate to strike out on his own in a solo practice, a career path that is all but unthinkable nowadays, given the increase in start-up costs and the crushing burden of student loans. Many older lawyers tell stories about how they were able to earn a full year of law school tuition by doing construction work or waiting tables during the summers between their years at law school. Those days are gone. Nowadays, a full-time construction job would not pay for a month of law school. There is no choice other than to incur massive debt as a law student.

Debt has a powerfully conservative influence. It prevents law school graduates from taking lower-paying public interest positions that serve the interests of consumers and poor persons. According to the National Association of Public Interest Lawyers, "Few graduates can afford to go into public service helping low income people protect their most basic rights."[20] Indeed, a recent survey of law school graduates from 117 schools found that two-thirds of the respondents were so deeply in debt that they could not even consider a career in public service.[21] This creates a disastrous choice: take a public interest job and default on your student loan, or take a law firm job representing powerful corporations you may not respect. This means that legions of law students are forced by simple economics to represent clients antagonistic to their sense of justice. There is ample money to be earned in representing big businesses, polluters, and white-collar criminals, but there is no money in representing consumers, crime victims, and the poor. Regardless of what law students would like to do in an ideal world, the current system forces them into jobs they resent.

All of this assumes that law graduates can obtain jobs in the first place, which is no longer a certainty. Recent statistics on the job market are not encouraging, and the situation is getting worse. The data suggest that only a fraction of recent graduates find jobs relatively soon after graduation. The old practice of lining up a job prior to graduation is now limited to students at the "top-tier" schools and to those students at less prestigious schools who are in the top quarter of their class. At "second-tier" and "third-tier" schools, the majority of students do not have a job lined up prior to graduation.[22] At these schools (that is, at the *majority* of law schools in America), the more likely scenario is that a student will graduate without a job, only to begin a grueling search for *any* legal job. Many recent graduates find themselves applying for any and all open positions, willing to take any legal job whatsoever in an effort to pay down their massive debt. Many recent graduates give up all hope for a paying job and either go back to school or provide free services in an "internship." Still others take jobs as paralegals and law clerks.

Recent law school graduates will be entering a profession that is becoming grossly overcrowded. The ratio of general population to attorneys was 700 to 1 in 1951, 400 to 1 in 1971, 300 to 1 in 1991, and getting worse every year.[23] Overcrowding creates a shark tank of bitter fighting over a limited pool of clients, which means that it is virtually impossible for a new attorney to venture out into a solo practice and compete with established attorneys. The old practice of "hanging out a shingle" is an anachronism. In most cases, there are virtually no options available to the young lawyer except to take a job with a private law firm, if such a job can be found. If a law school graduate takes a position with a firm having fewer than twenty-five lawyers, she will be paid less than $60,000, with a debt burden of nearly $1,000 per month, and with an expectation of having to bill nearly 2,000 hours per year if she wants to succeed.[24] Do the math: if this lawyer spends 2,500 total hours at work, she is making less than $20 per hour. That is a decent wage for a waitress at a nice restaurant, but it is far short of the lifestyle that most people associate with a professional degree.

Lawyers who are lucky enough to work in their chosen profession have to deal with the stark realization that the general public has a terribly low opinion of lawyers. A study commissioned by the American Bar Association found that lawyers had a mere 40 percent approval rating compared to 84 percent for teachers, 71 percent for doctors, and 79 percent for police officers; in fact, lawyers fared better than only two other professions—stockbrokers and politicians.[25] On the whole, lawyers are perceived as expensive, arrogant, aggressive, pretentious, and completely blind to any perspective beyond that which happens to favor their client at the moment. They are perceived as professional liars who are willing to take any position, however unethical or outrageous, so long as the client is willing to pay. To become a lawyer nowadays is to be simultaneously feared and despised.

To be sure, the public has always expressed a certain amount of distrust of and trepidation toward lawyers, extending all the way back to Plato's chastisement of "sophists" and Shakespearean characters who proclaim that we should "kill all the lawyers." Yet nobody can deny that the public perception of lawyers has taken a nosedive since at least the mid-1970s, when President Nixon resigned from the California bar under threat of disbarment, after most of his cronies (including Liddy, Dean, Colson, and Agnew) were disbarred for their involvement in the Watergate scandal.[26] More recently, President Clinton was stripped of his right to appear before the United States Supreme Court (and accepted a five-year suspension in Arkansas), while Hillary Clinton's law firm partner Webb Hubbell was disbarred after a conviction for fraud due to overbilling.

It is almost impossible to name a single public incident in the last two decades in which lawyers have generated good press for the profession. When the public hears the word "lawyer," three things may come to mind: (1) a criminal case that turns into a fiasco when lawyers dream up fanciful defenses that have no basis in reality, which happened in the O. J. Simpson case and the Menendez brothers cases in the 1990s; (2) a corporate implosion exposing business lawyers for setting up a byzantine Ponzi scheme, such as the savings and loan fiasco or the Enron debacle; or (3) a political dispute that devolves into a partisan shouting match, such as the Clinton impeachment or the decision by the United States Supreme Court that awarded the presidency to George W. Bush. In the wake of the presidential melee following the 2000 election, a commentator from CNN summed up the perspective of most Americans: "The big losers in all of this, apart from the American people? I vote for the lawyers. They have exposed themselves for what they really are: a bunch of smooth-talking used car salesmen who can take any words and twist them around so that they mean exactly the opposite of what they were intended to mean or exactly the opposite of what they meant five minutes earlier."[27] The willingness of lawyers to twist words into nonsense became quite clear when Alan Dershowitz, perhaps the most recognized lawyer in America, blatantly used statistics to lie in defense of his client, O. J. Simpson. At one point during the highly publicized trial, Dershowitz gave a public lecture in which he proclaimed that only one in a thousand battering husbands actually goes on to commit murder, suggesting a one-in-a-thousand chance that Simpson was guilty. He carefully left out a corollary statistic that was easily discovered by the press, namely that when a battered woman is murdered, the battering husband is the perpetrator in one-third to one-half of the cases.[28] After that farce of a trial, Dershowitz (a Harvard Law School professor, after all) turned to writing books and found himself accused of plagiarism—a charge against which he defended himself by blaming his research assistant for not checking original documents.[29] Another high-profile member of the Simpson team, F. Lee Bailey, was disbarred in Florida in 2001 and Massachusetts in 2002, and spent time in a federal detention center.[30]

The televising of courtroom proceedings that began in the late 1980s, largely at the initiative of cable television stations, was heralded as a democratizing step toward open government that would reveal lawyers as hardworking public servants. It did not work out that way. Instead, the high-profile cases coming out of California in the 1990s (the O. J. Simpson case, the Menendez brothers case, and the Rodney King case) showed that defense lawyers were willing to concoct all manner of groundless stories to absolve their clients of responsibility. The public disdain for how lawyers actually operate can be measured by the emergence of television shows with artificial courtroom scenarios from which lawyers are conspicuously absent, such as *Judge Judy*, *The People's Court*, and *Judge Hatchett*. The message of these shows is that lawyers must be kept out of the courtroom in order for justice to be rendered.

And yet while lawyers are highly visible in the news and on television, they are remote from the lives of ordinary people. Hourly rates of more than $200 for simple matters, going up to $400 for complex matters, guarantee that hardly anybody in the middle class can actually afford a lawyer. While O. J. Simpson, Claus von Bulow, and William Kennedy Smith can afford "dream team" lawyers such as Johnny Cochran, Alan Dershowitz, and Roy Black, most criminal defendants are given merely a cursory meeting with a low-paid, state-appointed lawyer, a few minutes before having to enter a plea in court. And while some lawyers will take cases on a contingency basis, the expenses of bringing a suit are so onerous that a lawyer will not take a case unless it is a slam-dunk winner, which means that ordinary injustice goes unremedied. For every toxic tort that is remedied along the lines of *A Civil Action*, there are scores of genuine tragedies that lawyers will not touch because the cost of bringing a suit against a large company runs into the hundreds of thousands of dollars.[31] All of this adds up to a situation of public frustration with lawyers, who appear out of reach while at the same time increasingly unavoidable.

The image problem is not restricted to litigation attorneys; corporate lawyers working exclusively on business transactions are equally suspect. For good reason, they are perceived as preoccupied with cooking up schemes to protect management at the expense of workers, or drafting one-sided form contracts that consumers cannot possibly understand, the type thrust upon unsuspecting citizens at every car rental counter and appliance superstore. Corporate lawyers have been at the center of every major economic debacle of the last quarter century, from the savings and loan bailout that cost taxpayers billions, to the Enron scandal, in which lawyers set up innumerable subsidiary corporations in tax-free havens for the sole purpose of committing fraud and avoiding income tax (Enron, the seventh-largest corporation in America, paid no taxes for several years).[32] When the scandal finally threatened to break open, Enron snapped into action and commissioned the law firm they had paid nearly $30 million in the previous year, Houston-based Vinson & Elkins, to conduct an "independent" ethics review of the legal structures that Vinson & Elkins had put into place. To nobody's surprise, the law firm absolved itself of wrongdoing. Weeks later, Enron became the largest U.S. company to declare bankruptcy, amid a congressional investigation into the violation of securities laws and possible tax fraud committed by the company and its accountants and lawyers.[33] The willingness of corporate lawyers to engage in shady deals and then disclaim responsibility shocked the federal judge who oversaw the savings and loan fiasco surrounding Charles Keating and his failed savings and loan:

> Keating testified that he was so bent on doing the "right thing" that he surrounded himself with literally scores of accountants and lawyers to make sure that all the transactions were legal. The questions that must be asked are: Where were these professionals, a number of whom are now asserting their rights under the Fifth Amendment, when these clearly improper transactions were being consummated? Why didn't any of them speak up or dissociate themselves from the transactions? . . . What is difficult to understand is that with all the professional talent involved (both accounting and legal), why at least one professional would not have blown the whistle to stop the overreaching that took place in this case.[34]

In light of these episodes, the overriding public sentiment about lawyers is that litigation attorneys are relentless pit bulls who twist the truth, while corporate attorneys are scam artists.

How have lawyers and scholars responded to this crisis? Have they sought the root cause of the problems? Are they willing to consider fundamental changes to the profession to restore its standing? Are they willing to rethink the traditional structure of law school, the bar exam, and law firm practice? What solution is being offered?

The response has been tepid and uninspiring. For the most part, lawyers have called for "professionalism" and "civility," and by recommending a return to the days when lawyers were gentlemen-scholars, statesmen, and esteemed brothers of the bar—assuming that such days ever existed in the first place. The subtext of this position is that the current crisis has its roots in a lack of professionalism among young lawyers and can therefore be remedied by spiritual means, as it were, instead of by making fundamental changes to the economic and legal structure of the profession. Literature in this vein draws from the formative role played by attorneys in founding the nation: nearly half of the signatories to the Declaration of Independence, thirteen of the first sixteen presidents, and most of the members of the Constitutional Convention were lawyers.[35] Anthony Kronman, former dean of Yale Law School, has called for a return to the model of the virtuous lawyer-statesman who places public service above the pursuit of money.[36] Sol Linowitz has made the same argument, claiming that lawyers have betrayed the profession by eschewing statesmanship.[37] Recent years have seen the creating of professionalism centers and civility codes.[38] This "professionalism crusade" adopts a shrill tone of high moralism and advocates an impractical return to an idealized golden age of legal practice, a time when, incidentally, the profession was less crowded and predominantly the province of propertied white males who could afford to adopt a tone of high civility.[39]

Demanding a return to professionalism is a pointless exercise when young lawyers lack the time, money, and job security to act "professionally." Given the expense and risk in becoming licensed and holding onto a job, lawyers today are *forced* by the system into being uncivilized, unprofessional, and nasty. Or to put the matter more bluntly, professionalism is a bourgeois virtue for those who can afford it. There is no chance to be a magnanimous Jeffersonian lawyer-statesman while operating under a crushing debt burden and immense pressure to bill insane hours, while facing fierce competition for clients and long odds for partnership. The call for professionalism is a simplistic solution to a multilayered problem. It is tantamount to attempting to solve the drug problem by telling kids to "Just Say No": it will not work because it does not get at the root economic and political forces causing the bad behavior.

The fact of the matter is that the practice of law is much harder than it used to be, especially in terms of the toll that it exacts on young lawyers. Consider the recent reflections of a 1960 graduate from Harvard Law School, looking back after forty years:

> Young Harvard lawyers are less content today than we were. They work harder, longer hours. They don't have the time to indulge themselves, to become Renaissance people. My classmates still believed that it was possible to go to plays—every night if we wished—to learn music, to have intellectual discourses. We led pretty decent lives in the law firms. Today, a Harvard graduate comes in conditioned to give up large parts of his life for a number of years. I don't know if it's a pretty decent life.[40]

A young lawyer in 1960 was expected to bill 1,500 hours per year and in return could expect partnership in six years.[41] A lawyer nowadays can expect to bill somewhere in the neighborhood of 2,200 hours for a 15 percent chance at partnership after eight years. Even then, he might be a partner in name only, not a true equity partner who shares in the profits, especially if he does not have a portable client base.

All of these factors add up to a nightmarish situation for young lawyers: a boring and expensive education; a crushing debt burden; a pointless but mandatory bar exam; exhausting jobs with little opportunity for partnership; shocking rates of anxiety, depression, and alcoholism; all amid an atmosphere of public hatred. What gets lost in the equation is the very thing that makes law attractive in the first place—the chance to use one's intellectual ability to secure justice for a client.

Endemic Unhappiness

There is no secret that the vast majority of young lawyers are deeply depressed and alienated. But here is an interesting and unexplored twist: lawyers hate themselves. In commenting on this, Scott Turow attributed such self-hatred to internalization of the public disapproval of lawyers, but in fact the problem is much deeper.[42] Attorney self-loathing is a specific response both to the conditions under which lawyers are educated, licensed, and regulated and to the economic cauldron into which they are thrown. Wholly apart from how the general public feels about them, young lawyers hate what they have become, what the profession has made of them. The end result is a double whammy—the public hates lawyers, and lawyers hate themselves.

Most young lawyers spend a significant part of each day fantasizing about ways to leave the profession. Just as a starving person will fantasize about food, or a homeless person will envision living in a mansion, lawyers fantasize about having the things that are conspicuously absent from their lives, such as balance and meaningful labor. Lawyers repeatedly fantasize about switching to a career involving something that they consider to be real, like teaching, psychotherapy, or running a bed-and-breakfast. When journalist Robert Kurson went back to his Harvard Law School reunion after ten years, he encountered partners at large firms confessing their desire to open a faraway convenience store or to be a clerk at Barnes & Noble. One alumnus was brutally honest: "I have fantasies about leaving [this job]. There's not a day I don't think about buying a cabin somewhere and just leaving it all. But I can't do it. I'm a pussy. You know, we didn't get into Harvard Law School by taking chances. Most of us are conservative. Except that being conservative is fucking killing me."[43] Most lawyers never act on these fantasies because they are paralyzed by the obligations that they have built up like so many trophies—family, home, cars, and so on—that they cannot afford to make a move, but also because the profession brainwashes them into thinking that any job lacking in money or power is unworthy of a lawyer, an indoctrination that begins very early when law school professors steer students toward large law firms. And so lawyers remain frozen, constantly telling themselves that everyone else feels equally depressed about his or her job. Yet on some level they know that this, too, is a lie.

There is a profound sense of resignation among lawyers, a sense that they have sacrificed their lives to do something they find unrewarding, as if they were serving time—an apt metaphor given the constant pressure to rack up billable hours. They do not say this out loud, but you can spot it fairly easily in their demeanor, their sighs, their disinterested gaze, and their narrow frame of reference that rules out anything whimsical or antiestablishment, not to mention the way that they immediately cross-examine and batter everyone in their line of sight at the slightest provocation, from loved ones to low-level employees. Among lawyers one finds a fatalistic sense that pain and sacrifice are to be expected in any job, and that suffering is inherent in work itself. My lawyer friends are always saying, "They call it *work* because it is unpleasant." As one young lawyer put it after taking a look at the senior partners at his firm,

> Somewhere toward the end of my first year with the firm, I had gleaned enough insights into senior attorneys' personal lives to know that I didn't want to follow in their footsteps. Simply put, few of them seemed happy. In fact, having succumbed to the pressures of practice over the years, most seemed bitter, frustrated, impatient and even hostile. I often sensed this from passing senior attorneys in the office halls, where the tension on even an average day could be palpable.[44]

Not surprisingly, when I listen to lawyers talk about their lives, I hear the sentiments of a broken and resigned people. Those at the very top of the pyramid are certainly well-compensated,[45] but their prosperity is built upon the immiseration of nearly everyone in the lower reaches of the hierarchy.

Tellingly, lawyers are happiest during the few hours before the start of the workday, when they take the time to read the paper, drink coffee, and exercise. Once the day starts, everything is downhill—the crush of boring and repetitive work, the reams of documents, the endless phone calls and petty negotiations, the ritualistic meetings and rote conferences that at first seemed so exciting but now seem so lifeless. At night they return home frazzled, with a sneaking suspicion that despite twelve hours of hard work, they have done nothing to make the world a better place.

If you watch lawyers closely, you will find that most of them have designed their workday so that it is peppered with little rituals to make the rest of the day vaguely tolerable, like leaving the office for a trip to Starbucks, scanning the magazines at the newsstand, or getting their shoes shined (something that lawyers do at an alarming rate). There is an aura of reverence to these rituals bordering on the sacred, although the actual content of the ritual is unimportant so long as it achieves the goal of getting one out of the office, making the lawyer seem like a convict who sits in tense anticipation of his thirty minutes of free time in the exercise yard. One can tell quite a bit about the profession by watching young lawyers at lunchtime, how they circle around repeatedly in search of some interesting distraction before getting back on the elevator to return to work with that sinking feeling in the pit of their stomachs, steeling themselves for another afternoon of watching the clock and secretly praying for some sort of natural disaster to strike the building, as a fifth-grader prays for a blizzard to close the school.

The lawyers I have known, even the successful ones, eventually come to view their work largely as a vehicle to generate money, and the actual practice of law becomes a nuisance that they tolerate to retain their lifestyle. They lose their intellectual interest in the law, and indeed they see the law as an impossibly complicated tangle of regulations, a jungle of confusion that (ironically) was created by their fellow lawyers. Once they lose interest in the law, they slowly shed the values that they previously held about service, community, and justice, and the resulting vacuum is filled by the mad pursuit of a portable client base, as each lawyer tries to polish his image and make himself attractive for clients. Lawyers in private practice eventually come to see the law as a mere game that they are lucky enough to know how to play, and for obvious reasons they quickly lose respect for the legal system and the rule of law. Among my classmates, the principal obsession is to stick in the profession long enough to earn sufficient "Fuck You Money" so that they can one day say "Fuck You" to the firm and then walk away without going broke. But the incremental accumulation of "Fuck You" money often takes so long that the young lawyer ends up, well, fucked.

Over the years I have passed through many law offices in many cities, only to see the same mysterious aura of quiet desperation, low-level conformity, and replaceable men (and now women as well) who resent their lives, their partners, their families, and their fate. To a person, lawyers whom I meet at social occasions tell me in flowing prose about how much they enjoy their practice; and just like clockwork, the same lawyers pull me aside and confess how unhappy they are and how great a mistake they made by becoming lawyers. I know how this feels because I experienced it daily—at times I felt that my office might as well have been a high-tech prison cell with wall-to-wall carpeting for all the freedom that it offered. On most days, my arms began to feel like molten lead and my head was weighed down by a horrible heaviness, a cloud that no amount of coffee could clear. Ten times a day I caught my thoughts drifting toward a better life, some sort of pathway out, then I got up and went to the bathroom just for the excuse of leaving my office.

The air of disappointment, regret, and longing running through the lives of many, perhaps most, young lawyers is so pervasive that it is silently assumed between lawyers when they meet, so that they do not even talk about it, just as lepers probably did not spend their time talking about the vagaries of leprosy. There is a morose quality to their lives, and they have a masochistic outlook that seems to welcome suffering and disappointment as if it were built into the fabric of life. Having given up any hope for an interesting and fulfilling life, they expect others to feel the same way, so that when they see successful people in nonlegal professions such as business or the arts, they experience a strange combination of jealousy and the desire to see that person punished. The feeling is similar to that expressed by a mediocre insurance salesman in George Orwell's *Coming Up for Air*: "I got the job and . . . the job got me . . . Everything that really matters to me happened before that date."[46] Yet, by the time most lawyers realize how truly unhappy they are, they are already stuck so deep that any sort of career change is unthinkable. The demands of the practice exert a heavy toll, but this toll is unnoticeable because lawyers do not explode; rather, they implode, aging at an alarming rate, swallowing their rage and decaying from the inside out as they suffer through heart attacks and ulcers. Beneath the tight-lipped, Protestant work ethic facade is hollowness.

How did this happen? Is it inevitable? Can it be fixed?

In this book I will argue that the causes of this unhappiness run very deep, stretching all the way back to the first day of law school and extending through the bar exam and the first years of private practice. These are the years that I will be examining in these pages, years that are exciting in their own way, yet also emotionally crippling and destabilizing for the majority of lawyers. To my mind, the young lawyer who emerges through this hazing ritual usually comes out deformed. To be sure, there are a few lawyers who are happy and fulfilled, who find a niche for themselves and manage to balance a challenging career with an exciting personal life. But they are a noticeable minority. It is possible to meet lawyers who love what they do, serve the interests of justice, and lead a healthy and integrated life—but it is rare. How rare? An ABA study of young lawyers found that more than 70 percent of practicing lawyers complained that they were required to endure intolerable daily pressures and tensions, while 50 percent claimed that workaholic schedules left too little time for themselves and their family.[47]

Let us be very clear on the question of causality: the legal profession makes lawyers unhappy. We must reject any suggestion that lawyers are unhappy *prior* to their immersion in the legal system, that these unhappy people somehow self-select their own unhappiness by subconsciously placing themselves in a depressing profession.[48] This assertion is not borne out by the statistics, since law students enter law school with the same incidence of mental problems (including depression) as other graduate students, yet emerge with elevated mental problems. And furthermore, college students usually lack information about the legal profession and often have no idea what law school entails. It is true that most of us in the profession were high achievers, perfectionists, and neurotics from the beginning, but these are common traits of successful people in all fields. We did not bring a cloud of depression to the profession; we discovered the cloud when we got here. In other words, the problems affecting young lawyers are predominately systemic, not personal.

When lawyers describe what they enjoy about their careers, they tend to focus on external factors such as the relatively high salary and the prestige of being a professional. When describing their lives, lawyers rarely invoke internal goods such as the ability to help others, the intellectual challenges of law, working with concepts and ideas, and so on. While these are present to some degree, they are somehow overshadowed and often destroyed by the commercial demands of the profession. And it is also the case that lawyers often lie to themselves and others about their feelings. It would be a mistake to take lawyers at their word when they claim to be motivated primarily by the intellectual challenge and the service component of their practice, because whenever they can find a reason to avoid the nuts-and-bolts practice of law, they will inevitably do so. I have observed dozens of lawyers who built a successful practice to the point where they faced a choice between "rainmaking" and continuing to practice law, and in each instance they dropped the practice of law like a hot potato. This suggests that the practice of law is not satisfying apart from the money it brings, an inference that is confirmed by the fact that lawyers readily leave the practice of law whenever they can make the same money without practicing law. This also suggests that the profession needs to be redesigned so the practice of law is not something one endures like a bad movie, but is instead intellectually interesting and challenging.

Objective and Subjective Measures of Unhappiness

There are two different types of data on lawyer unhappiness, which we might call *objective* and *subjective*. These correlate to third-person and first-person perspectives on the problem. The *objective* material consists of empirical studies and hard figures on lawyer dissatisfaction, such as surveys conducted by bar associations and statistics culled by researchers. By contrast, the *subjective* material consists of first-person accounts of lawyers' unhappiness, describing their hopes and fears, their aspirations and disappointments.

Some researchers place their trust in objective data because it purports to be more scientific, less biased, and less impressionistic than subjective first-person accounts. At the other extreme, some people prefer to work with the subjective data because it strikes closer to the actual experiences of flesh-and-blood individuals. It is my belief that both types of material (objective and subjective) need to be taken into account to get a full picture of young lawyers, so in this book I present both statistics *and* confessional narratives from young lawyers. In most chapters, the objective and subjective material will be mixed, but the reader should keep in mind that they are merely two ways of documenting the same phenomenon. By analogy, a social scientist might study the Great Depression both by looking at statistics on the economy and by listening to people tell stories of what it was like to live during those times.

The objective data that we will be examining on lawyer dissatisfaction are deeply troubling.[49] As noted earlier, a study from Johns Hopkins University found that lawyers rank worst out of 104 professions when it comes to depression;[50] one survey found that greater than 40 percent of associates at New York City law firms plan to leave the profession at some point; and another survey found that 70 percent of California lawyers would not become lawyers again.[51] Many lawyers are leaving the profession based on their negative experiences in private practice,[52] and those who stay are reporting incidents of alcoholism, suicide, and depression at levels much higher than the rate of the general population.[53] Amazingly, researchers have found that only about 10 percent of entering law students have symptoms of psychological problems, but the number jumps to 40 percent by the end of law school, which suggests that unhappiness has its roots in law school (indeed, law students are consistently more anxious and depressed than their counterparts in business and medical schools).[54] Just looking at the numbers alone, the picture that emerges is one of a shrinking and overly competitive job market for young lawyers, plus widespread dissatisfaction among those lucky enough to obtain legal positions.

But the numbers tell only one side of the story. The other side is the actual experience of flesh and blood people who struggle to keep their sanity and dignity while immersed in a social practice that is becoming increasingly harsh and unrewarding. To get a full picture of young lawyers, it is necessary to reveal the world as they see it, to explain their hopes and frustrations. To accomplish this, I have written many of the following essays from my personal point of view as a young lawyer in the belief that my impressions will resonate with those who have been through the same experiences.

The Six Causes of Lawyer Unhappiness

In light of my assertion that the legal profession is to blame for making lawyers unhappy, I have identified six distinct causes of dissatisfaction among young lawyers, each of which will be treated in a different chapter.

The *first* cause is law school, which by all accounts is a major ordeal. I have never met a person who liked law school. Period. And the amazing thing about law school is that it teaches so little in exchange for subjecting law students to a grueling mixture of fear, anxiety, and tedium. Law school does not empower or transform the students in an intellectual sense, nor does it provide rudimentary lawyering skills. The main thing that it teaches is the ability to read appellate opinions from the perspective of a reviewing court, to bluff and pose under pressure, and to be litigious. It subtly trains lawyers to be apolitical and socially conservative. Indeed, I can still hear the advice of a law school professor on how to succeed: "Litowitz, you will need to attract clients, and the only way to attract clients is to make yourself more, not less, conservative than they are."

The *second* cause of unhappiness is the bar exam, a ridiculous, pointless, and outdated rite of passage serving no practical purpose. Ostensibly created to protect the public by ensuring that lawyers possess basic knowledge, the bar exam does not inculcate quotidian skills such as drafting pleadings, drawing up contracts, or representing a client in court. The true function of the bar exam is more sinister. First, it is a way for existing lawyers to protect their client base by regulating the flow of incoming lawyers (in this way, it functions as a tariff or entrance fee). Second, it serves an ideological function by scaring future lawyers into subservience to the state bar authorities. It accomplishes this by making the young lawyer feel so lucky to pass a surreal exam and join the ranks of an elite group of licensed professionals that she represses any critical stance on the ordeal and forgets that she just spent three months learning a bunch of arcane rules and test-taking skills that have virtually nothing to do with the practice of law. Having seen how intrusive and arbitrary the bar authorities can be, the young lawyer is hesitant to challenge them once she receives a license.

The *third* cause of lawyer dissatisfaction is the transformation of law into a business that pretends to be a profession. Law firms are increasingly modeled on profit-driven corporations, where a concern for the bottom line takes precedence over every other facet of practice. In the maddening crush for profits and billable hours, everything that was scholarly and noble about the practice of law becomes quantified, and each person is judged numerically. Eventually, law firms morph into high-tech factories where one class of lawyers (the legal bourgeoisie) exploits another class (the legal proletariat), and the profession splits into the haves and have-nots. The class of young lawyers ends up scratching and clawing for the client portfolios controlled by an elite cadre of older lawyers. In the new world order of law firms, young lawyers are given the label "associate," the same term used by Wal-Mart to describe minimum-wage workers. And the comparison is apt, because young lawyers have the same lack of job security. I conclude that being an "associate" is tantamount to being a wage worker employed at will.

The *fourth* cause of lawyer dissatisfaction is the pressure upon lawyers to practice in a law firm setting instead of as a solo practitioner who can set her own limits on acceptable behavior. Sociologists have long pointed out that groups are more ruthless than individuals, and this holds true for law firms, which have somehow picked up the worst excesses of group-think and crowd dynamics. Large law firms are like the military, where obedience to authority and technical proficiency is fetishized and where the lower-level players are instructed to follow orders. When practicing in a firm, the young lawyer picks up the dirty tricks which transform law into a game of power and economic hardball, not justice. At first, there is a burst of empowerment that comes with the mastery of a new skill and the ability to have an impact on the lives of clients, but this soon degenerates into the sobering realization that the side with the most money and political power always wins, and that most cases are resolved in a particular way because of political influence or the ability to outspend the other side. The "law-firming" of the profession has turned lawyers into rapacious predators who have shed the restraints of individual conscience. But since law school graduates do not have the skills or financing to start their own practice, they inevitably gravitate to law firms and pick up these negative traits.

The *fifth* cause of unhappiness is the struggle with the technological changes that have made the practice of law less humane and increasingly mechanized. In many cases, lawyers are now isolated atoms sitting alone in their offices, surrounded by machines and endless piles of paper, subject to constant monitoring. The law office has become an electronic sweatshop and the lawyer has become what Marx called "a mere appendage to the machine."[55]

The *sixth* and final cause of unhappiness is mental dysfunction. Like abused kids who develop multiple personalities as a coping mechanism, young lawyers learn to split off their true self from a false lawyer-self that relies on instrumental rationality and nit-picking. Slowly, the false lawyer-self colonizes the true self, which becomes dissociated. This is why so many lawyers complain of not quite feeling themselves. The separation of an individual and her professional role is not automatically bad, so long as the deeper self is able to find fulfillment and realization in the performance of the professional role, and so long as there is some critical distance between one's self and the role. But for lawyers, the split is often total: their non-lawyer selves completely disown their professional selves, and the two sides fail to integrate. The false lawyer-self speaks in legalese while the true self looks on helplessly in shame at what the other half of its personality is doing. Even worse, some lawyers respond to this dissonance by merging with their false selves, losing all critical distance. It is exceedingly rare to find a lawyer who is comfortable with both her individual and her professional identities.

The attorneys whom one meets on a daily basis are caught in a deadly cycle of worrying about attracting clients, trying to bill a superhuman number of hours, keeping one step ahead of tricky lawyers on the other side, and feeling paranoid about being sued for malpractice. It hardly sounds like a worthwhile life. For most practitioners, being a lawyer is like walking in quicksand through a war zone, thick and groping, with a veneer of fake civility caked over the entire process. Almost by accident, one adopts a mindset that is frightening and alienating, and one no longer recognizes oneself.

The problems that I have set forth are very deep, but they can be minimized with the appropriate reforms. The practice of law does not have to be so disappointing for so many people; it *can* be a rewarding profession. I hope that genuine progress will be made by showing the system at its worst, by showing that things need not be the way they are, and that they can be fixed with the right attention. Because I believe that social criticism must have a positive component, I end each chapter with a set of recommendations for remedying the cause of unhappiness discussed in that chapter. I truly believe that these suggestions can make a difference and improve the profession, even though I fully recognize that the radical reforms advocated in this book will not find many adherents. As always, the very people and institutions with the most power to fix the situation have the least incentive to do so.

The Methodology of Social Criticism

Criticizing the legal profession requires the overturning of a vast network of unchallenged myths that buttress the existing regime. These myths begin on the first day of law school and continue throughout one's career. They send the message that things must be as they are, that the existing order is natural and inevitable, and that any attempt to change it is irrational, radical, utopian, or illogical. This is how the powers that be (law schools, bar examiners, bar associations, law firms, and judges) insulate their power, with a false claim of necessity and with unjustified appeals to the "common sense" that they have manufactured and thrust upon young lawyers. Our first order of business is to dispel and expose the distortions and myths that stand in the way of rational social criticism. After all, it was precisely under cover of these myths that the legal profession became such a disaster. Just remember: it is perfectly acceptable for you to question *everything* about the way young lawyers are educated, socialized, and trained. Do not buy into the rationalizations that have been offered to you. Think for yourself. If you truly agree with me that the profession has completely failed young lawyers, then you will need to support some very radical reforms.

For example, law students have been told that they need three years of courses taught by Socratic method in order to prepare for the practice of law. But why? Why *three* years instead of two? Why not courses taught by group projects? Why isn't there a mandatory apprenticeship component? Why are students ranked by GPA, and why are students ranked at all? Why are law schools ranked, and who benefits from the rankings? Why are students required to learn ancient rules (such as the rule against perpetuities) but are not required to study legal problems of poor people? These are a few of the questions that you should be asking.

Law students are told from the first day of orientation that they are about to enter a "noble profession." Most students silently assume this to be true. But where is the proof? Why is the practice of law more noble than, say, architecture or medicine? Calling the profession "noble" insulates it from criticism. Who would dare to reform a "noble" profession? I suggest that we speak the truth by acknowledging that lawyers are no more noble than other people, and in fact may be less trustworthy and less commendable than nonlawyers.

Consider the bar exam. Why does it exist? Most lawyers will balk at the suggestion that the bar exam should be abolished. Surely, they say, it would be unimaginable for the profession to operate without a bar exam. Yet they flounder when told that Wisconsin does not require a bar exam for in-state lawyers,[56] and that the bar exam is a relatively recent invention designed in large part to keep foreign-born lawyers from becoming licensed (in fact, Justice Oliver Wendell Holmes never took a formal bar exam, according to a noted legal historian: "Judge Lord of the superior court appointed two examiners; they separately asked Holmes a few questions; Holmes answered the questions, paid his five dollars, and was admitted to the bar").[57] Here as elsewhere, we sometimes need a reminder that many of our practices are contingent and irrational. Maybe we should abolish the bar exam altogether, or change it to a pass/fail workshop on the skills of a first-year lawyer. Perhaps the existing regime serves only the sinister purpose of erecting a roadblock to the profession, and is held in place by self-appointed experts who do not really care about young lawyers.

These are difficult questions for lawyers to ask, partially because young lawyers have been brainwashed to avoid asking such questions, but also because there is a large reward potentially awaiting those who hold their nose and accept the system. No one has an incentive to undercut the system that *could* make them wealthy. And we cannot expect older lawyers to raise a finger to help. Highly paid lawyers with a fair amount of power are not going to be motivated to initiate the reforms that I propose in this book, such as revising the law school curriculum or abolishing the bar exam, since they have lived through these ordeals and have emerged on the other side. In fact, they have disincentive to improve things for the next generation of lawyers, since they now stand to benefit by making the road more arduous for those who could enter the profession and compete with them.

The practice of law runs sweet and sour in a way that cuts off rational criticism—it offers enough carrots to make one forget the sticks that are landing on one's back. But the effect of this process is to insulate the profession from serious criticism, since the negative aspects are absorbed by the positive. A beautiful example of this process is offered by critical theorist Herbert Marcuse in his description of how the positive side of an experience can outweigh the negative:

> I ride in a new automobile. I experience its beauty, shininess, power, and convenience—but then I become aware of the fact that in a relatively short time it will deteriorate and need repair; that its beauty and surface are cheap, its power unnecessary, its size idiotic; and that I will not find a parking space. . . . In a way, I feel cheated. I believe that the car is not what it could be, that better cars could be made for less money. But the other guy has to live, too. Wages and taxes are too high; turnover is necessary; we have it much better than before. The tension between appearance and reality melts away and both merge in one rather pleasant feeling.[58]

This process happens time and again when lawyers think about the legal profession. They think to themselves, "Yes, law school was a nightmare in which I learned next to nothing, but it was a fair price to pay for my present station and salary," or "True, the bar exam was totally absurd and useless, but now it's over and I have my license, so I never have to think about it again," or "The pressures of legal practice and the hostility and competition are overwhelming, but this is inevitable and cannot be changed, so I should focus on the money that I am making and reconcile myself to working within the system as best I can." This is the thinking of compromise, rationalization, and submission, even as it parades as pragmatism and maturity. The key to improving the system is to capture and isolate the critical thoughts before they dissolve into grudging acceptance.

The purpose of critical inquiry is to show that our existing arrangement is biased and that our customary way of thinking is distorted, that our social practices and institutions can be rationally reconstructed. The first step in this process is to recognize that many of the myths and stories that we tell ourselves about the legal profession are simply wrong, that they are rationalizations and excuses. Literary critic Roland Barthes explains how the critical process requires subverting the myths and institutions that have come to appear naturalized and reified: "[M]yth consists in overturning culture into nature or, at least, the social, the cultural, the ideological, the historical into the 'natural.' What is nothing but a product of class division and its moral, cultural, and aesthetic consequences is presented (stated) as being a 'matter of course'; under the effect of mythical inversion, the quite contingent foundations of the utterance become Common Sense, Right Reason, the Norm, General Opinion."[59] This book follows the critical tradition by exposing the dominant myths and rationalizations (the "common sense") that props up the legal profession. This type of critique should not be confused with a Nietzschean or deconstructive "trashing" that depicts the system as rotten to the core, without offering an alternative. Instead, the purpose of critical theory (and the purpose of this book) is to assess our current beliefs and practices and to explore the alternatives, to imagine a better world.

My project is *diagnostic* and *restorative*—to explain how the legal profession is riddled with problems, and to suggest ways that we can reform it for the better. Unfortunately, most lawyers are so busy keeping up with the demands of the profession that they have little time to reflect upon it, putting them in the same position as Kierkegaard's bookseller who never stopped to consider the meaning of his life until the morning that he woke up dead.[60]

Since the road to unhappiness for young lawyers begins in the first days of law school, that is the topic of the next chapter.

chapter two:
The Trouble
with Law School

After more than a decade, the mere mention of law school still leaves a bitter taste in my mouth. And I am not alone. When my ex-classmates get together, the conversation inexorably loops back to what a difficult experience law school was for all of us, even for those who excelled and seemed successful during those years. A good friend is fond of paraphrasing Dickens about the three years of misery we endured: "It was the *worst* of times, it was the *worst* of times."

Most law students do not understand why they feel so unhappy, although every one of them feels disaffected and troubled to some degree, even if they do not admit it to others or even to themselves. A person caught inside the whirlwind of law school is oblivious to his condition, much like a psychotic who cannot see how crazy he is. It does not take a degree in psychiatry to spot the abnormal mental conditions created by law school, because the symptoms are apparent in any first-year classroom: the constant release of nervous laughter, the shaking legs and hands, the palpable anxiety and quick breathing, the release when someone else is called on, the endless tics and obsessive rituals used by the students to ward off their fears, the colored pens and outlines clutched like religious icons, and the crossword puzzles or computer games for the bored students sitting beyond the professor's firing range.

Even for those who manage passably well, there is always a looming specter of depression, weight gain, reliance on caffeine during the day and alcohol at night, daily mood swings, and bouts of anger and frustration, not to mention boredom and resignation. Some people can thrive in this environment, but they are a minority. For most students, law school is something that must be tolerated, a necessary evil that they would rather forget.

Since the pressures of law school are so intense and draining, students rarely have the time or inclination to step back and think about what's wrong with the system, and most don't really care as long as they get through with a degree in hand. In truth, law students have been taught so little about what the profession is really like and about what skills they will need that they have no idea what their education is lacking, or even that law could be taught differently if some thought were put into it. As a result, most students treat law school as a hazing ritual to be endured, a bizarre rite of passage to be suffered as the price for getting the degree. But law school could be so much more, and therein lies the great waste of time, money, and talent.

As a law student, I did not understand quite what was happening to me, but I knew that something was very wrong, not just with me personally (I admit that it was a difficult time) but with the entire structure of law school, the whole ball of wax—the way that classes were taught, the social milieu, the student-faculty relations, the curriculum, the orientation of the placement office . . . *everything*. As a law professor who has taught at several law schools and made a careful study of how they operate, I have a pretty good idea of why law school is troubling to so many students. Perhaps my reflections will help today's students articulate their own experiences and sort out some of their feelings, or at least let them know that they are not alone in finding the experience so depressing.

Law School Is Traumatic, Not Inspiring

One thing that we know with certainty about law school is that it *breaks* people, that it is experienced as a trauma, an assault. Like other traumas, when it is actually taking place it is overwhelming and very difficult to understand. Only after it is already finished can it be pieced together in retrospect, like a robbery victim who later tries to reconstruct the features of an assailant. When I say that law school *breaks* people I mean that almost nobody comes out of law school feeling better about themselves, although many come out much worse—caustic, paranoid, and overly competitive. From outward appearances, the students churned out by the law school machine are shiny and bright, with a professional no-nonsense attitude, but inside that shell lies a nagging hollowness.

First-year law students are forever saying that law school suffers in comparison with college, a comment that law professors attribute to laziness, on the theory that students preferred college because they were not pushed as hard. This interpretation completely misses the students' point, which is that law school suffers in comparison to college because it is not a *transformative* educational experience. In college (and even more so in graduate school) one learns to identify and pursue one's interests, to evolve, to build, and to get to know oneself better, leading to a feeling of empowerment and self-assurance. In comparison, law school is like high school, complete with a dictatorial classroom milieu and numbing attention to minutiae and petty rules.

Law school is not *transformative* because it does not engage the students on an emotional or intellectual level. Stuck in large classes, pitted against a mob of others, reading boring cases about nameless and faceless people day after day, law students resign themselves to three years of memorization, tedium, and rote learning. Unlike the comparatively loose atmosphere of college, where students participate in discussion groups and ask questions during class, in law school the professors have absolute power and unquestioned status while the student is a second-class citizen instead of a partner in learning.

Notice how a successful college student identifies herself by her interests and skills; she says things like, "I am an art major with an interest in working for a museum," or "I am a chemistry major hoping to work on polymers." All of that comes to an abrupt stop in law school, where students learn to drop their personal interests and engage in a memorization contest that rewards formulaic thinking and rigid rule-following. Law students rarely identify themselves by their area of interest (e.g., "I want to practice tax law," "I am interested in admiralty law"), but instead identify themselves by the social ranking and the pecking order of where they want to practice (e.g., "I want to work at a big firm," "I think I can get a job working for the City," "I can't get a job doing transactional work, so I have to settle for personal injury law"). There is a cynicism to this transformation, an admission that law is uninteresting in its own right and that it cannot be pursued intellectually but only as an instrument for earning money.

At the elite law schools, the transformation happens in the first year, as the students sign up for interviews at large corporate firms without really having any interest in corporate work apart from the salary and the corresponding respect that it brings in the eyes of others. In law school the students become obsessed with their standing relative to other students: it is no longer a question of doing what one wants, but rather of doing what other people want. Or to put the matter concretely, Mr. X wants a job with the large firm to impress Ms. Y, who covets the same job, but Ms. Y covets that job in the first place because she thinks that Mr. X covets it, and so forth in an endless and inescapable circle where everyone is competing for the same prize even though no one can articulate why they want the prize in the first place. This was true in my own case. Despite being something of a free-thinker and rebel with left-leaning inclinations while in college, I found myself in a summer internship at a large firm, under the rationalization that "it couldn't hurt to get some legal experience." And so my career path had been set in motion, almost automatically. A year earlier I could not have named five firms in Chicago, yet after a year of law school I was like a robot who could unconsciously register the appropriate level of admiration or condescension at the mention of a law firm's name.

Students come to realize, from listening to gossip and from the law school career center, that the profession is hierarchically arranged with big firms at the top and small firms at the bottom, and with corporate law at the top and family law (and public interest work) at the bottom. All of this is in the air, as it were, floating around the law school, much as gossip careens around a freshman dormitory. As if by magic, the law students are suddenly hooked up with firms through a kind of courtship and mating ritual based on profuse representations and promises that will never be kept. Especially at elite schools, the school itself is simply a holding pen for the big firms. This suits the big firms recruiting fresh bodies, and it also benefits the law schools soliciting huge gifts from the firms. What gets lost in all of this is the arduous task of placing students in jobs suited to their particular idiosyncrasies and temperament.

At the same time that law school *breaks* students, it also *creates* them, or rather, molds them in its image. But what does it create? On the positive side it creates people who have good reading and writing skills, who are diligent and hardworking, who can see both sides to an issue. Law students are hard workers, and they are typically very high achievers with above-average intelligence. But on another level, law school churns out some very scared people who have learned during their first year of law school how to bluff and fake their way through an intense interrogation. Law students are trained to appear polished and quick-witted, with a response to any question, but this surface pragmatism belies lack of depth and the nagging suspicion that they have not been taught enough to keep them afloat if they were let loose to practice law. So at the same time that they are taught to act empowered, they are truly disempowered because they cannot practice law unless put into an established institution and given instructions. Despite the appearance of professionalism and self-sufficiency, law students are actually helpless and dependent when they graduate.

The First-Year Fiasco

A study in the *International Journal of Law and Psychiatry* pointed to clinical evidence that entering law students are no more prone to depression than the general population, but that by the time they graduate, law students are overwhelmingly more depressed than the general population.[1] Standing alone, this statistic is a stinging indictment of law school, a clear indication that something is terribly amiss. But this statistic will come as no surprise to anyone who has endured law school, since every law student knows firsthand that it is all too accurate. And indeed, the study has been repeated and confirmed.[2]

Even more telling, studies indicate that law students are significantly more depressed than their peers in medical, dental, or business schools.[3] This statistic is indeed surprising. Why should law students be more depressed than medical students, who suddenly find themselves making life and death decisions? And why should law students be more depressed than *business* students, whose work lacks the political and social dimensions that make law so interesting?

The explanation lies, I think, in the way that law students are taught. Unlike their peers in medical and business schools, law students do not spend any time on group projects planning how to help clients. Instead, they are taught the law by memorizing a huge load of doctrines and cases divorced from the lawyer's social role as an advocate or helper. Business students and medical students work with case studies and hypothetical situations where advice can make an immediate difference in someone's life—the doctor solves a pressing problem and relieves suffering, while the business student helps build a solid future for a client by marketing a product or recalibrating a firm's finances. In contrast, law is inward-looking; there is no "client" when one learns the law, so the student feels that he is working in a vacuum. The student's social world consists of an antagonistic and distrustful relationship with a distant professor who merely tolerates the student's existence, and a series of temporary and always competitive relationships with fellow students, relationships that erode at a moment's notice on the most trifling pretense, leaving a student stranded without a support group.

There is no necessary reason for law to be taught in a way that is so divorced from real people with real needs. Law *could* be taught through the use of clinical practicums or case studies. In passively memorizing case holdings and statutes day after day, the law student loses sight of the potentially active side of law, where a lawyer can solve problems and affect people's lives directly. Law school is *voyeuristic*—the student stands outside the arena and watches what other lawyers and judges have done in the past. This conveys a subtle ideological message that lawyering requires the bracketing of personal involvement with a cause, that emotion will permanently disable one's reasoning ability. As master trial lawyer Gerry Spence reflected on his legal education, "In the cases I read in law school and since, passion was treated like some crazy step-sister locked in the closet. The law had no relationship to living, suffering persons. Law was business. And business was served by law."[4] The high level of emotional detachment created in law school does not necessarily breed superabundant reasoning ability. Rather, it breeds boredom and disinterest, which are useful for lawyers who need to distance themselves from the effects of their actions, but crippling for those who insist on finding meaning in their work.

Much of the blame for the depression among law students lies in the way law is taught during the first year, namely by the Socratic method. The first-year classroom is usually an immensely large class in which the students are not told in advance what questions will be asked of them, but know that sooner or later the cruel hand of fate will summon them to be called on to perform in front of their peers. Without receiving grades until the end of the semester, the students' entire sense of achievement is wrapped up in their classroom performance. In other words, everyone's mastery of the material is suddenly made public at a moment's notice, and each person is watching the others and measuring himself against them. This arrangement can be empowering for those with public speaking ability, but it has a tremendous downside for the vast majority who see no need for the fear of public humiliation to be used as a Sword of Damocles to motivate them. In my own case, I can recall lying in bed panicking over whether I was going to be called on the next day, and trying to figure out in advance what questions the professor was going to ask. This was time that could have been better spent working *with* the professor instead of seeing him as an inquisitor.

The Socratic method is really a ritual of subjugation that purposely disables the student. Its main purpose, its *raison d'être*, is to keep pushing the student until she gives in. There is no way to prepare for a public performance that is so one-sided, in which the student is asked impossible questions designed to trip her up. And there is a strong element of sadism in the Socratic interchange. For example, my criminal law professor used to walk around the room to ensure that he was standing directly across the giant hall from whomever he was questioning, to create the greatest distance. I'm not sure what he hoped to accomplish with this tactic, but he succeeded only in creating more physical and emotional distance than was necessary to teach criminal law. The tactic provided absolutely no pedagogical benefit, and in fact some of us were so scared by it that we never bothered to meet the professor outside class.

It is not clear what the Socratic method prepares students for. Ostensibly, it is supposed to replicate the courtroom experience, but honestly, I don't know any lawyer who has found himself in a room with a hundred of his peers watching him, being forced to defend himself against questions that he cannot possibly answer, thrown to him by someone who knows the answer but won't tell him. In the real-life practice of law, lawyers can prepare well in advance of a court appearance, and feel solid about their answers before being grilled by a judge. In fact, there are no situations in the practice of law that are comparable to being called on during the first year, which is why the first-year experience doesn't prepare students for *anything*. Again, it serves no *pedagogic* purpose.

Why, then, is the Socratic method so popular? First, it is cheap because it can be used to teach large numbers of students. Second, it uses fear and shame as a motivating force, which is easier than motivating people with ideas and worthy goals. Finally, it has the deceptive appearance of rigor, because it frightens the students into preparation, and this fear is then mistakenly interpreted as dedication. The crucial point is that the Socratic method does not challenge students intellectually: all it does is frighten them with public humiliation, and it is this fear of humiliation that motivates the students to overprepare and spend all night worrying. A better system would focus the students' anxieties on the legal work itself and not on the grilling that they might receive in tomorrow's class, by giving them challenging projects and expecting quality work from them, by giving them time to prepare before making a presentation.

In any event, the anxiety that students feel in law school is wildly out of proportion to the importance of the material they are learning. To see my point, simply ask this question: Is it really necessary to raise the anxiety levels of ninety students just to teach the parole evidence rule?

As someone with a Ph.D. in philosophy, I can report that the "Socratic method" was not used by Socrates to teach large audiences of students. Socrates used this method only as a rhetorical device in his conversations with a few friends. The method worked like this: Socrates would ask a friend for a definition of a concept, say, "Justice" or "Truth." Socrates would then show that the proffered definition had all sorts of problems. For example, if a friend defined "Justice" as "Giving people what they are owed," Socrates would poke holes in the definition by asking, "Would you give a knife back to a deranged man if it was owed to him?" This process would continue until Socrates had exhausted his friends' definitions, at which point he would often present his own theory of Justice, Truth, or Beauty.

The Socratic method was a rhetorical device for conversations, not a method for teaching a subject matter. This needs to be repeated: Socrates did not use the Socratic method to teach a particular topic, such as law or medicine. And, in fact, a moment's reflection makes clear how cumbersome and downright absurd it is to teach information using this method. Can you imagine an introductory-level literature or philosophy class where the professor constantly walked around asking questions of the students? Self-respecting college students would shun that class like the plague, for good reason—the *teacher* is the expert, and he should be the one teaching. The method is even less appropriate for teaching practical subjects like law and the legal system, which are intrinsically complicated to such an extent that students need a professor who makes the subject *less* complicated, not more. Yet somehow law students get so disoriented that they lose their common sense and come to accept this strange way of teaching.

I can still vividly recall the way that my Contracts professor delighted in the Socratic method and made a big production of unfolding a gigantic and meticulously prepared seating chart with each person's face on it. Without offering a shred of explanation about the subject matter that he was supposed to be teaching us, he would say, "Ms. Jones, what were the facts in *Hadley v. Baxendale*?" To this day, I can recall my rage at the situation. This esteemed professor made no effort to introduce his subject, no attempt to teach by writing on the blackboard, and no attempt to empathize with how nervous we felt. This was supposed to show how hard-core he was, but it came off as callous and unfeeling, not to mention pedagogically unsound. Years later I thought back on that classroom, and I asked myself why the professor didn't stand up in front of the class on the first day and provide a simple overview, such as:

"This is a course on contracts. A contract is an enforceable promise to do something or to refrain from doing something. There are many types of contracts—some are *express*, some are *implied*, some can be oral and some must be in writing. A contract generally must have certain elements, such as an offer, an acceptance, a meeting of the minds, and consideration. In this course we will be examining the different types of contracts and the various elements of a contract. Our first case deals with whether a contract can be implied under certain circumstances. The reason we are reading this case is to give us an idea generally of what a contract requires in the eyes of a court, and to see if a court will find a contract to exist even if there is no express agreement between the parties. I am now going to choose a name at random and ask that person to help us by explaining the facts of the case. I know that this is new to you, and so I will try to be supportive and help you to understand how the facts of a case should be explained."

This would have been wonderful as a way of framing the course and defusing our worries. Instead, he came off like a macho drill sergeant and alienated everybody.

Most law students realize by the second week that the entire first-year arrangement is something of a sham, that the students themselves could teach the class using the Socratic method, and that the professor didn't really *write* the textbook, he simply tied some cases together with a few discussion questions and a few exercises to be pulled out in an emergency. The truly curious and enterprising students often find out that their professors have not been very successful in practice, which is a further cause for concern. After a few weeks, the students do not really see any point in coming to class, since they can get most of the material by cramming at the end of the semester, or by studying on their own. Nevertheless, they are compelled to show up because most law professors take attendance, which is a terrible throwback to high school, and frankly counts as an admission that students would not otherwise show up.

I can still recall with absolute clarity the first time that I was called on in Contracts, early in the first semester. The professor asked me an oblique question, "What did the appellate court judges *see* in this case?" I had no way of knowing, since I had never studied appellate advocacy and had never worked for a court or a law firm that did appellate work. So I took a guess: "The briefs of the parties . . . ?" He never said whether I was correct, but instead went on to quiz me about the citations in the footnotes of the case, which were Greek to me at the time, including references to the American Law Reports, the Restatements, arcane English reports, and so forth. Whenever I couldn't explain a citation, he would ask sarcastically, "Why didn't you look that up?" I couldn't really explain that I didn't have the time to look up every citation that appeared in every footnote since I had to read ten cases the previous night and each had fifty citations that I couldn't understand. So I just shrugged and let sit the implication that I was lazy, when in fact I had studied for hours and briefed the case in detail.

The exchange seems trivial, but when you are in front of a hundred of your classmates it is very difficult to endure. And the amazing thing is how little *teaching* is involved in the process. What I learned from this and countless other exchanges is that I should study very hard, not because the material was interesting or because I would master an important subject, but because it would protect me if I were called on in class. Eventually, then, students come to study defensively, as if warding off the fear of being publicly shown to be deficient. This is very different from studying out of interest or concern for the subject. Indeed, one could generalize and say that law students study not because they are interested in the materials, but because they are warding off lower grades, or because they want to get on law review, and so on. Very few actually study out of an interest in the law, largely because the law is not presented to them as something with intellectual appeal.

One absurd thing about the first year of law school is that professors are asking the students things that the professors should be teaching in the first place. I must admit that I never adjusted to having a professor ask, "What is the message of this case?" when he or she was the expert and I was a mere novice. It comes down to laziness, really: instead of teaching in the classic sense, the professor expects the student to look up everything himself and essentially teach himself the subject. And for all their bombastic talk about theory and ideas, most professors end up testing on the black letter of the law, which is why law students turn to commercial outlines for a clear explanation of the topics that their professors have been dancing around all semester.

All of the absurd, topsy-turvy drama of the first year can be found in that overrated movie, *The Paper Chase*, which is still considered the quintessential law school movie. There is a scene in which the awe-inspiring Professor Kingsfield addresses his first-year Contracts class at Harvard by saying, "Your minds are full of mush. I am here to teach you how to think."[5]

This has always struck me as extremely grandiose. Imagine telling the brightest students in the country that they cannot think clearly because they have not yet learned the highly specialized language of the law. Through the movie, the protagonist (the indefatigable Mr. Hart) gradually pieces together the doctrines of contract law and eventually comes to respect Professor Kingsfield, although from where I stand Kingsfield is undeserving of respect. After all, Kingsfield is completely reckless in his treatment of the students, he is overbearing and takes delight in ridiculing the students, and he hides the doctrines so that the students have to assemble them from scratch, essentially teaching themselves contract law. The pretense of the movie is that Kingsfield's abusiveness (his distance, sarcasm, and hierarchy) are actually a token of quality and intellectual achievement. This appears to me as a giant rationalization and whitewashing of a horrible figure: I would respect Kingsfield more if he simply taught the subject in a clear way and showed empathy for the students. Instead, we are told that his cruelty is actually a type of kindness, his deprecation a form of respect. In this version of the Stockholm Syndrome, a man's cruelty is not only accepted but esteemed by the very people whom he has harmed. This process gets repeated during the bar exam, as students develop respect for the bar examiners who are putting them through hell.

The same thing happens in *One L*, in which Scott Turow witnesses a brutal interrogation on the first day of class. When the student explains to the professor in front of a hundred peers that the case is about a man who died "intestate" (without a will), the professor asks if that has anything to do with the intestines or the testicles, and then tries to trap the student into a series of mistakes and misstatements. Turow sees the interrogation as evidence of a sharp mind, but I would question how much intellectual fire-power it takes for a seasoned professor who has spent decades on a subject to humiliate a twenty-something student on the first day. In any event, much of Turow's book is devoted to the traumas of the classroom experience in the first year, which leads to the inescapable conclusion that far too much time is wasted by forcing students into an immediate situation of disempowerment. As Turow remarked, "For me, the primary feeling at the start was one of in-credible exposure."[6] This type of experience has led one clinical psychologist to comment that students tend to overidealize professors, spending an in-ordinate amount of time endlessly speculating about them, "a phenomenon that rests upon the authority they exercise over the students' fate."[7] It is a dis-turbing dynamic based on an unequal power relationship, which hardly makes for an ideal learning environment.

The Case Method and the Loss of Context

The second-biggest mistake of law school (the first being the Socratic method) is that law is taught inductively, by reading one case after the next until they slowly build up into a coherent body of law (or more accurately, until some type of organization is imposed on them). Teaching in this way is often called the "case method," and there are two problems with it. First, it does not prepare students for the practice of law, in which lawyers do much more than simply read cases individually and then assemble them into a mo-saic, so law school provides an impoverished view of legal practice. Second, by reading endless cases, students become unconsciously disposed to resolv-ing problems with litigation and expensive appeals, since they spend all day reading about disputes settled in the appellate courts. This is a dangerous double whammy: students do not learn to solve problems through negotia-tion and discussion, and they are told that disputes can be handled with ex-pensive litigation. No wonder they come out ready to fight at the drop of a hat. This message—that the practice of law inevitably involves litigation and appeals—is a mistake. In fact, if lawyers are doing their job correctly, very few matters should be resolved by the appellate courts. For example, most trans-actional lawyers would be ashamed if they handled a transaction that had so broken down that the dispute reached litigation, let alone an appeal.

The case method is not the only way that law can be taught, but it is probably the cheapest, which again is one reason that it goes hand in hand with the Socratic method. Historically speaking, the case method is a recent experiment in legal education, being less than one hundred years old. In early times, lawyers were taught rudimentary legal concepts at law school and earned their credentials through apprenticeships where the law was imbri-cated in actual disputes. In other words, they received on-the-job training in the real world. All of this changed with the revolution in legal education brought about by Dean Christopher Columbus Langdell of Harvard Law School, who in the late 1870s argued that law should be taught "scientifically," the same way that one would study an organism. Just as one studies an organism cell-by-cell, one must study the law case-by-case. Langdell earned his keep as a consultant to other lawyers and not as a practicing lawyer in his own right; he was appointed dean at Harvard Law School despite his lack of experience, and he immediately set about to recreate legal education in his own image, pushing for the hiring of professors that had little practical experience.[8] The very appointment of Langdell at Harvard was itself a bold departure from hiring experienced practitioners to teach the law, as one commentator observed in his history of the Harvard Law School: "For the first time in the life of Harvard Law School, it was proposed to choose as Professor, a young man of no legal reputation (except among the few lawyers who had employed him), a man of no national fame, and a lawyer who had substantially no court practice."[9] What Langdell could offer was a new vision for teaching the law: his claim to fame was the notion that we should break down areas of law into their component parts and study them piece by piece, much as a biological organism could be broken down into component systems (digestive system, nervous system, skeletal system), all the way down to the level of individual organs and cells. In a similar manner, the body of civil law could be broken down into components of torts, contracts, and property, and then further divided into subsystems such as offer, acceptance, consideration, breach, and damages, such that each of these topics could be analyzed "scientifically" by looking at cases dealing with them.

Instead of actually giving the students a contract to look at (heaven forbid!) or even a preliminary overview of the types of contracts they will encounter in practice (oral, written, implied), the modern curriculum throws students into the mix at the cellular level, forcing them to read innumerable case decisions without having any idea where the cases fit into the overall picture of the law. This amounts to teaching by induction, the slowest method available, and by constantly looking at individual trees instead of the forest. As a result, most students are totally clueless for most of the semester until they purchase a commercial outline and finally discover the overall structure of the material that they have been assigned so far.

In an address from 1886, Langdell summarized what students would receive under the case method, using remarks that seem bizarre today: "[Students will receive] not experience in the work of a lawyer's office, not experience in dealing with men, not experience in the trial or argument of causes—not experience, in short, in using law, but experience in learning law; not the experience of the Roman advocate or of the Roman *praetor*, still less of the Roman *procurator*, but the experience of the *jurisconsult*."[10] This is a tautology: law students should be trained to be law students. Certainly, law students would be better served by learning how to *practice* law, because that is what they will be doing for the rest of their lives. In any event, by roughly 1910, Langdell's method had been firmly ensconced as the dominant teaching paradigm in law schools, creating the existing regime of boring and heavy casebooks, Socratic inquisition, and the practice of losing students in minutiae and depriving them of primary legal materials. This has been the dominant method of instruction for so long that hardly anybody has any workable ideas of how to improve on it, although most critics will admit that it drives students crazy with boredom.

The main problem with the case method is that law students have no sense of the big picture. For example, they begin law school by reading cases in a torts casebook without being told what a "tort" is; they read about contracts without seeing an actual contract. They must build their understanding of law piece by piece instead of being provided with a framework during the first weeks of school. The lack of an overview is particularly troubling, since it appears to the students that the faculty are willfully hiding something from them. In my own case, I can remember coming to the realization during the second week of law school that civil actions differed from criminal actions in two ways: a criminal action is brought by the state and requires proof beyond a reasonable doubt, while a civil action is usually between private citizens and requires a preponderance of evidence. None of my teachers had bothered to explain this simple distinction, having instead thrown us into a whirlwind of case decisions without any sort of overview about how civil and criminal law were distinct. Here I was, at an elite school, having to teach myself the most basic principle of the American legal system.

I can also remember the epiphany that I had at the end of my first month of law school, when I realized that the law was implicated in everything around me. I was walking to get a hamburger for lunch when I realized that my purchase of the hamburger was basically a contract. From there I began to realize how law affected everything, how law played a part in the construction of every building that I passed on the street by virtue of zoning and property laws, how the criminal law protected me from others, how property law divided the land, and how the law was an evolving code, like a DNA structure shaped over the centuries by precedents. None of my teachers had bothered explaining the grandeur of law; instead, they threw tons of cases at me, forcing me to slog through minutiae and miscellanea night after night. If I studied the material well into the night, I could finally grasp how the law professor approached the subject, which still left me pretty far removed from the actual content of the law. Or, as Scott Turow put it, "[L]aw school does not teach students to think like lawyers. It teaches them to think like law professors."[11]

The second problem with the case method is that it ignores the social context (and the *legal* context) in which a dispute arises. Students are made to focus on one minor issue of a case without actually seeing the underlying documents that led to the conflict. For example, in the first-year course in contract law, students are not asked to do any of the things that a contract lawyer does (meeting clients, drawing up agreements, negotiating, amending documents, reviewing documents, brokering disputes), but instead are taught to adopt the judge's perspective, as someone looking down on the dispute in a detached way. The case decisions that law students read arrive without any description of the burdens endured by the litigants, or the economic and emotional toll of a lawsuit. All of the interesting social context is bracketed and the students end up dissecting reams of cold, hard legal opinions.

Students should spend more time doing what lawyers actually do to help their clients, not reading about situations that have spun so far out of control that the parties needed judges to sort things out. Reading what a judge has written provides little guidance on the question of what lawyers do from day to day, and it goes without saying that students will graduate to be lawyers, not judges. Think of how absurd it would be for medical students to spend three years reading about the work of other doctors, but never actually working on patients themselves. Or, as Judge Jerome Frank put it, the case method is tantamount to "future horticulturists studying solely cut flowers."[12] Law school takes this absurdity as a three-year program of study, from which law students emerge without the slightest ability to perform rudimentary tasks like forming a corporation, drafting a trust, or even filing a lawsuit. I can still recall my own embarrassment during law school when a neighbor asked me to draft a quick bill of sale for the purchase of a rather expensive item at a garage sale; I was stupefied as he asked, "What have you been doing in law school?" The truth was that I had never seen a bill of sale. Similarly, Alan Dershowitz confessed that he was already an established professor of criminal law at Harvard Law School when he decided to represent an actual defendant, and found himself totally clueless:

> Having made my decision, I did not have the foggiest notion of where to begin. They didn't teach that sort of thing in law school. (Now I try to.) I turned to one of my former students, Harvey Silverglate, who had been practicing criminal law in Boston for four years. He urged me not to try to handle a case like this alone, gently reminding me that I barely knew how to find the Federal Courthouse and had no experience in preparing the necessary pre-trial motions and complying with other such technical requirements. He offered a role-reversal: he would become my teacher for this case. I willingly assumed the status of student, and we got down to the hard work of preparing a defense.[13]

What an amazing story—a professor relying on a student to teach him how to practice law!

Another problem with the case method is that students get the mistaken impression that law practice is characterized by careful legal argumentation, when in fact most cases are determined by which party can spend the most money and delay the longest. All of the background power plays are erased in the court's opinion, as if the case arrived at the appellate court denuded of history and meaning. Law professor Pierre Schlag brilliantly captures how law students adjust from the case method to the real world:

> For our students, the transition is extremely abrupt. For three years, the talk is of bringing law in accord with purposive reason. . . . Rudely, however, these three years are brought to a close by the vulgar reality principle of the bar exam. This is quickly followed by one (quite possibly) last, exceedingly hedonistic vacation. This vacation typically ends badly with the law student finding himself confined in a small cool cubicle with a window, a couple of diplomas, one potted plant, and a very bad view. From that cubicle, law begins to seem far less genteel, far less intellectualized, and most of all, far less respectful of its own inner normative text than it did in law school. In that cubicle (and in tens of thousands like it), the student-become-lawyer will learn and learn quickly that law is a power game.[14]

I suppose that the one skill taught in law school is the ability to analyze a stack of case decisions, since this represents the bulk of what law students spend their time doing. But amazingly, even within this narrow range of activity there are severe limitations to what students can do. For example, students learn to read individual cases, but only in legal writing class do they perform the lawyerly skill of organizing these cases into a linear line of argument for a client. In law school, students read a case as if they were mini-judges of some higher court, straining to determine if the lower court made the right decision. This is good preparation for being an appellate judge, or perhaps a judicial clerk, but it is not central to what lawyers do every day.

If law were taught by some other method, perhaps students could be given large-scale assignments that would teach real skills—for example, a Corporations professor could have students draft paperwork to form a corporation, draft a shareholder agreement, draft a lease for business offices, draft a promissory note and security documents for borrowing money, and so on. These would be real skills. Instead, students read case decisions about corporations (something that actual corporate lawyers rarely do) and then sit down at the end of the semester to face an impossible and ridiculous hypothetical question which counts as 100 percent of their grade. This way of teaching and testing rewards memorization instead of creative solutions, which is why the best law students are often history majors who have learned to cram disparate pieces of information into their head, memorizing every rule and every exception.

Even if law school was perfectly adept at teaching case analysis, this would still leave untaught the remaining legal skills such as drafting wills, negotiating leases, setting up corporations and partnerships, reviewing contracts, and so on. As the majority of lawyers in this country do not focus exclusively on litigation and do not spend all day reading cases (let alone briefing them!), there is little to be gained by subjecting law students to three years of reading cases, except to give students a super-specialization that will be of little use in practice.

Part of the explanation for the narrow focus on case law can be traced to the background of law professors, most of whom come fresh from Ivy league schools, judicial clerkships, and a few disappointing years at a big firm. These young men and women spent three years of law school reading cases, and did more of the same during their judicial clerkship. By the time they get appointed as a law professor, there is not much else they know how to do. Without any other frame of reference, they quite naturally set about replicating the only system they know.

No discussion of law school would be complete without acknowledging that faculty-student relations are totally regressed to the high school level: the teacher is all-knowing and all-powerful, and takes attendance. In this scheme, the student is dependent, weak, vulnerable, and clueless. This power differential is accentuated, not lessened, by the Socratic method and the case method. As a result, students spend an inordinate amount of time and energy speculating about their professors and dreaming of ways to placate them. This is a hierarchical, top-down relationship that does not facilitate mutual growth.

The cruelty and hierarchy of the system are slowly internalized by law students. This can be seen in how they gradually shift their allegiance from "soft" teachers to "hard" teachers. In the first-year curriculum, students encounter two types of teachers: the hard teacher and the soft teacher. The hard teacher is usually male, well-dressed, with a formal air bordering on the pretentious, and makes a habit of grilling students with impossible riddles and bizarre hypothetical cases as if stumping his students was a mark of great pedagogy. He is quick to use rhetorical devices such as ridicule and sarcasm, and he often aligns himself with the more established wing of the local bar, such as commercial lawyers. The prototype of the hard teacher is Professor Kingsfield in *The Paper Chase*, who continually reminded the students that they *might* have what it takes if they only learn to think exactly the way he does. The hard teacher is initially fearsome, but offers the promise of respect and protection for those students who withstand his aggression and find a place within his hard-nosed universe.

In contrast, the soft teacher usually wears slacks and a blazer, and is somewhat disheveled. He is almost apologetic about the difficulties of learning law in the first year, and he goes out of his way to provide some sort of overview for the students to ease their anxiety at being called on. The soft teacher is often a liberal and a reformer, and he takes a less draconian view of the law than the hard teacher: he is more open to policy arguments and more inclined to see the law in a historical or social context.

Law students make an immediate determination as to which of their professors are hard and which are soft. As the first year gets under way, the students form an initial attraction to the soft teacher solely on the basis that the soft teacher will not ridicule them and is making an effort to teach. They have an extreme dislike of the hard teacher who appears as a punishing father figure or a withholding and barren mother. As the school year wears on, many students come to see the soft teacher as wishy-washy and wimpy, and their allegiance tends to shift toward the hard teacher. This switch occurs because students slowly begin to accept the flawed notion that the hard teacher is a better teacher simply because he is hard. Almost imperceptibly, students come to believe that the hard teacher represents rigor and thoroughness and that the ridicule and sarcasm dealt out by the hard teacher were really a stroke of kindness designed to shock the laconic student into the real world of lawyering. At this point, the students look back on the soft teacher as too focused on policy arguments and too afraid of hard rules of law. This shift in identification and affection from the soft teacher to the hard teacher is very important because it illustrates how students come to accept (indeed, to respect) character traits that are offensive. It is simply wrong for a teacher to motivate students by fear and by sarcasm, but by the end of the first year the students come to see this actually as a form of affection, which is precisely how some battered women come to feel about their abusive husbands as the result of a similar mixture of dependency, fear, and identification with the aggressor.

In any event, students quickly learn that law school involves three years of variations on the same theme: sit through boring classes, go home every night and read a few statutes, look over four or five cases for each class, makes notes in the margins, and prepare a standardized synopsis of the case and a "policy" analysis of the decision (e.g., Did the court adopt a rule that is economically efficient?). This settles into a three-year routine that nobody would describe as invigorating or intellectually stimulating.

Law school grading is another source of unnecessary frustration. Grades are experienced as almost totally arbitrary. In my own case, I could never predict what grade I would get based on how much studying I did. To prove this point, a classmate who lived in my law school dorm performed a very interesting experiment. During the first semester he spent the same amount of time preparing for each of his finals—civil procedure, contracts, torts, and property. At the end of the semester, he gave me the news: "You won't believe it: I got one of each, an A, B, C, and a D. It makes absolutely no sense."

Given that most law students are high achievers whose performances on exams are roughly equivalent, there is little meaning to grades in any event, and the entire system should be replaced with the Yale-style grading scale of "high pass, pass, low pass." Instead of distinguishing themselves based on a few thousandths of a point on a GPA, students should be given academic credit for unique projects that would highlight their potential, such as becoming involved in actual cases through the law school clinic, writing a law review article, working for a legal organization, and so forth. Unfortunately, law firms are too lazy to judge students on their own merits, instead adopting rigid GPA guidelines. The law schools should resist this brute classifying of law students according to their numbers, but in fact law schools go one step further and provide information on class ranking, thereby turning the law school into a pure caste society.

As a law professor, I can report that the raw scores on most exams are clustered in the B/B+ range, with a few As and couple of Cs. If you plotted the raw scores on a chart, it would look like an extremely narrow isosceles triangle. We then have to take these raw scores and recalibrate them according to a totally artificial curve that separates the scores to make them appear spread out. This has nothing to do with reality and everything to do with creating a bogus ranking of the students so that they can be easily sorted and plucked by law firms.

Part of the problem with law school is that professors do not know what role to adopt. Very few of them can be considered dedicated *teachers* in the strict sense of an individual who wants to impart knowledge to others. Instead of actually teaching subjects, they bluff and pose and hide the ball. If they are not teachers, then perhaps one would expect them to be *scholars*—but even this is not the case. Most legal scholarship (as it appears in law reviews) consists in gathering immense amounts of research and then drafting a mundane restatement of the law overrun with footnotes. So, if they are not teachers and not scholars, then perhaps they are *practitioners*. But here, too, it turns out that many law professors never practiced law or were not very successful as practitioners. This leaves them in a kind of netherworld. They are not teachers in the strict sense of persons devoted to pedagogy, they are not scholars in the sense of persons with doctorates who are devoted to high theory, and they are not practitioners in the sense of practicing lawyers who are involved in the nuts and bolts of the legal profession. Instead they are some bizarre mixture of all three roles. This is reflected, of all places, in how they dress—neither formal nor informal, neither academic nor professional, but within a nondescript and unassuming middle ground. These people (non-scholars, non-practitioners, non-teachers) have made law school in their own image, and they continually replicate this image by hiring people who mirror them.

How Students Lose Their Social Conscience

Law school has a strange way of taking bright, ambitious young students, many of whom are interested in social issues, and changing them into apolitical and cynical beings who want only to make money. This transformation is obvious to anybody who spends time around law students, and it is borne out by the statistics kept at elite schools like Harvard, where 80 percent of entering students express a desire to practice public interest law, but only 5 percent make good on this commitment at the end of three years.[15]

The exact mechanism of this transformation is something of a mystery, but there is no denying that many law students lose their social commitments in a hurry. This transformation was the subject of an interesting memoir of a Harvard graduate:

> From 1986 to 1989, I was a student at the Harvard Law School. I entered committed to public-interest law, but after three years I came within one day of joining the vast majority of my classmates in practicing law at a large corporate firm, a career which I, along with most of them, would find lucrative, prestigious, challenging, and ultimately unsatisfying. . . . We came to law school talking about using the law as a vehicle for social change, but when it was time to decide what we would do with our lives, we fell over each other to work for those law firms most resistant to change.[16]

One explanation for this transformation is economic: law students simply cannot afford to take public interest jobs. The President of the American Bar Association admitted in 2000 that law school graduates typically had upwards of $80,000–90,000 in debt, and the average public interest position paid $32,000.[17] Using these figures, a young lawyer with a typical debt load was spending $1,000 per month on debt repayment for ten years, leaving approximately $1,000 net per month to cover rent, food, car, insurance, medical, and all other expenses. There is no reason to suspect that these figures have shifted in the favor of young lawyers over the past five years. This means that a typical law school graduate who takes a public interest job can hardly afford to pay her rent and put food on the table.[18] And while some law schools now have loan repayment assistance programs to help students who take public interest positions, these programs do not have a proven track record. As a result, many students will take a public interest position only if they have no other options, and then switch to a large firm whenever they get the chance.

The high level of debt among law students pushes them not only into the private sector, but into the most conservative, high-paying positions. Even the mid-level jobs are problematic, since recent graduates will still have difficulty paying down their debt if they take a small firm position paying, say, $50,000. In an amazing concession that the economics of law school are simply unbearable, the dean of Nova Southeastern University Law Center in Fort Lauderdale has flatly admitted that an average student taking an average job cannot manage an average debt load, acknowledging that students at his fourth-tier school (who have little chance for a big-firm position) often leave campus "with their J.D. degree in one hand and a note for $100,000 or more in education loans in the other."[19] A debt of this magnitude is basically a home mortgage without a home.

But economics is only a partial explanation for the conservative trend within law schools. The other part of the equation is the subtle training, shaping, and funneling of law students' vision into a gradual disdain for public interest work as too low-paying and too dirty for members of an elite profession. There is no other way to explain why persons such as myself underwent such a radical transformation during the first year of law school, suddenly learning how to "play the game" and get a high-paying job at a big firm. Looking back, I cringe at having told recruiters that I wanted to practice corporate law when I really had no idea what that meant, apart from the fact that everybody seemed to speak about corporate lawyers in reverential terms. In effect, then, law students are trained to desire something they do not really understand, solely because it commands a high salary. Anybody who goes to law school can name countless classmates who begin the year as offbeat characters, perhaps with long hair or an earring, only to end up sporting a new look and seeking a job at a big firm. Surely law school has complicity in this transformation—it teaches students so little about the practice of law and the different options available to them that the students can see only one way to measure their options, namely in terms of money.

Another factor at work in the eroding of social values is the generally anti-intellectual atmosphere at law schools. Although the law school classroom passes as a forum for ideas, the actual spectrum of discussion is narrow, running from middle-of-the-road left to middle-of-the-road right. In three years of law school, I never had a professor who espoused any radical view of the left or right, either socialism or libertarianism. In this way, law school pushes students into the middle of the road, into the larger culture where money is the ultimate value.

Part of the problem is the way that the first-year curriculum is artificially divided into contracts, torts, criminal law, and property. This division is ideological and expresses a value judgement about the subjects that a lawyer ought to know. This way of breaking down the law into subdivisions could be replaced with a different curriculum that might be more empowering to the students. For example, the first-year courses could be divided into "public" matters such as criminal and constitutional law versus "private" matters such as contracts, torts, and corporations. It could also be divided into "theory" and "practice," with half of the year devoted to skills courses. My point is that the existing curriculum is the result of a choice, one that subtly conditions the students to value certain areas of law over others. For example, notice how poverty law and family law are marginalized at most law schools, whereas commercial and corporate law are required courses that appear on the bar exam as well.

One of the few things that law students actually learn in law school is how to market themselves. Of course, this is mostly packaging, but there is something to be said for the ability to present oneself. However, beneath the luster is fear, precisely because the students haven't learned the mechanics of law practice, so they only *look* like lawyers. In other words, they emerge totally dependent on others, like a child. Deep down, the central fear of every law student (I felt it myself) is that they will be discovered as a fraud, a phony, someone who dresses the part but who knows nothing, who will be exposed at any moment, like a graduate of medical school who cannot take a pulse. This sets the tone for the fronting and fakery which will be expected of the lawyer in the future. To this day, when I hear lawyers bluster with their phony tone of self-assurance and pretension, I know that it can be traced back to law school.

My point here is that students arrive in law school with unique and idiosyncratic career goals, but over the course of the first and second years all of this changes, as individual aspirations are replaced with a one-size-fits-all stampede toward the large firms. Gradually, the bulk of the student body comes to develop the same goals and the same interests—to serve large companies, to have a nice house and a nice family, and to endure what it takes to become firmly ensconced in the lumpen yuppietariat.[20] At times, these people are troubled by the nagging sense that this path was not of their own creation; they missed the chance to be truly autonomous. This is precisely what troubled the conformist judge depicted by Tolstoy in *The Death of Ivan Illych*, who on his deathbed wonders how his life could seem so wrong when he did everything that was proper in the eyes of other lawyers and judges:

> "Maybe I did not live as I ought to have done," it suddenly occurred to him. "But how could that be, when I did everything properly," he replied. "If I could only understand what it is all for! But that too is impossible. An explanation would be possible if it could be said that I have not lived as I ought to. But it is impossible to say that"—and he remembered all the legality, correctitude and propriety of his life.[21]

This is the reaction that lots of young lawyers have when they obtain prestigious jobs at top firms; they did everything that they were supposed to do, so they cannot understand why they are so unhappy. They cannot believe that the legal profession is so discombobulated that it delivers its *winners* into a condition of misery.

Law student conservatism is also caused by the method of instruction, which systematically teaches students to distrust their own sense of justice. This is a subtle process, but it starts in the first days of law school when students are told that their initial reaction to a verdict is primitive and irrational because it has not been filtered through the silken web of legal ratiocination. The entire first year is a kind of brainwashing in which students pick up a new way of thinking—"thinking like a lawyer"—which is possible only by suppressing their previous "thinking like a regular person." Students are systematically taught to distrust their own feelings as naive, unrealistic, utopian. Consider the advice of a law school graduate who published a popular book containing "survival strategies" for law students: "Check your common-sense reactions to the law and law school at the door. This will lower your levels of frustration. Law school is sometimes counterintuitive. In other words, there often seems to be no logic to it at all. The Rule? Don't expect everything to make sense. Sometimes nothing will. Let go of your 'logical way of thinking.' Stop thinking like a layperson. You are no longer a layperson. You are a lawyer-to-be. Think like a lawyer."[22] In other words, you will need to forget that the whole point of law is to render justice.

Duncan Kennedy, a professor at Harvard Law School and a founding member of the Critical Legal Studies Movement, offers a brilliant account of how students are trained to distrust their own sense of justice through an endless diet of what he calls "hot" and "cold" cases. The hot case is a case that riles up the emotions because a seeming injustice has been committed (Kennedy's example of a hot case involves an Appalachian family kicked off their farm by a mining company). The students' sense of justice is offended by the verdict in the hot case, but the law professor tells them that their initial reaction to the case was pre-legal and knee-jerk, that if they only knew the law they would see that the court's ruling was justified by some higher principle such as freedom of contract, the need for clear liability rules, or economic efficiency. The cold case is an extremely boring case where a dry rule of law is announced by the court and the student reacts with dispassion. The students learn that they were wrong to react to the hot case out of moral indignation, and they make a mental note to treat cold and hot cases alike; that is, dispassionately. This routine sends the message that "emotion will only isolate and incapacitate you. The choice is to develop some calluses and hit the books, or admit failure almost before you begin."[23]

In the end, most students view the legal system as a sham, a naked power play. They start to believe that judges can rationalize any result in any case and then call it "legal," that all law is simply politics, and that at the bottom there is no logic whatsoever to the law and no way to criticize an opinion as unjust. I can vividly recall getting this message from my tax professor, who said, "Tax law has no logic whatsoever and the entire scheme is unreasonably and insanely complex, with no reason for most provisions other than political bickering and compromise." This is the perspective that most students adopt toward the entire edifice of law. They emerge from law school already full-blown legal nihilists who think that the whole thing is just a big debating game in which lawyers should switch sides depending on who is paying them, much like Henri Sanson, the executioner of Paris, switched employers after the French Revolution, executing his former bosses.

If you doubt that law school has a conservative influence, ask yourself whether you know any law students who became *more* radical in law school. If you look closely, you will see that virtually all students undergo a change in their clothes, hair, jewelry, and demeanor during law school, and this change usually involves a move away from the left and toward the middle or the right. It is true that one must conform to some degree to function in society: long hair and dirty blue jeans seem out of place in a court of law. But while *some* conservative shift is to be expected, the shift among law students is simply too strong, too fast. Lawyers emerging from law school at age twenty-five already have a mannerism, style, and demeanor more appropriate to a person of forty-five. Speaking for myself, I immediately distrust these polished kids who tell me with a straight face and no hint of irony that they want to be an expert in commercial or corporate law. They seem a little bit too pat in their responses, too eager to sacrifice themselves for a large impersonal institution.

Another factor in making students more conservative is the influence of the placement office at law schools. It is impossible to exaggerate the extent to which placement offices favor private practice over public service. When I was in law school, each law firm had a special folder containing shiny promotion materials, whereas the public interest file was located quite literally beneath the corporate files, in a dusty cabinet. Students quickly got the message that law firms offer a safer environment than government jobs and public interest work. It goes without saying that students pick up their teachers' disdain for public interest jobs, as represented by the tilt of the curriculum to business interests instead of courses on poverty and race relations. Students who wish to enter public interest law have to look long and hard for a mentor on the faculty.

How Things Could Be Different

The best paradigm for how law could (and should) be taught is the first-year course Legal Writing and Research. This course teaches practical skills, with a low student-teacher ratio, using writing assignments based on practical problems. As things stand, Legal Writing is the one course that approximates what lawyers actually do. All classes should be taught to some degree in this manner, with group projects that tie into actual court cases with real clients from the law school's clinic. Each project should have a moral dimension, with the students explaining how their action harmonizes with the ethical rules of the profession. This can be accomplished by switching to the case method of instruction currently used in business school or by having students work on teams to accomplish a particular task (drawing up an estate plan, forming a corporation, filing a lawsuit), or both.

Second, the Socratic method should be abolished. In its place, teachers should use a combination of lectures and problem sets, letting the students learn concrete tasks like drafting agreements, filing complaints, and taking depositions. The old practice of assigning five cases every night and then having the students cram with commercial outlines should be avoided at all costs.

Third, law school should be shortened to two years of classes and a one-year apprenticeship in which students work with practitioners, and then return to school to explain their projects. Lawyers should be asked to visit the classrooms and present scenarios that they deal with on a day-to-day basis, so that students have some idea of the social implications of their work. This involves making law schools more practical and less intellectual, but that is no great loss because law schools were never very good at challenging students intellectually in the first place.

Fourth, the present system of grading and class ranking should be abolished. Students should be ranked on the scale of high pass; pass; low pass. The present grading system has no positive pedagogical purpose—it exists mostly to divide the students into groups so that they can be plucked by law firms based on a single quantitative criterion. Law firms are already too focused on numbers and outward signs of prestige—there is no point in encouraging such one-dimensional thinking.

Fifth, the curriculum should be changed significantly to emphasize practical skills and to make students aware of the needs of poor persons. Law schools should require courses in poverty law and public interest practice, or courses on "legal problems of the poor."[24] This might create some sympathy for the vast number of people who are without job security, health care, and legal representation.

In the end, law school creates so much anxiety, so much looming fear and humiliation, so much competition, and so much raw boredom that law students feel chewed up and powerless. This system benefits everyone except the law students. It does not *have* to be this way: things could be different, classes could be more interesting, more actual skills could be taught, students could work in teams to solve problems. We will know that we have succeeded when law students are no longer reporting levels of depression and anxiety so far above those of students in business school and medical school.

Some of these reforms are being implemented, slowly but surely. For example, a criminal law seminar at the University of Pennsylvania is currently drafting the criminal code for a small foreign nation, and several professors in the area of corporate law are shifting toward the case studies method used in business schools.[25] But the prospects for widespread reform do not look good, for the simple reason that the deans and the professors (and the law firms) are heavily invested in the existing structure. *They* excelled in law school, and so they have simply recreated the same environment and cloned themselves, like a mutant strand of DNA. They recreate persons just like themselves, who are really only qualified to create persons like themselves, and so on forever.

But as bad as law school is, it only leads to a more bizarre experience: the bar exam.

chapter three:
The Pointless Ritual
of the Bar Exam

The bar exam is a charade that should be abolished or radically reformed. It has no pedagogical purpose and it does not ensure that lawyers possess rudimentary skills. Ostensibly designed to protect the general public by ensuring that lawyers have minimum qualifications, it fails to provide any protection because the material on the exam is arcane and unrelated to the ability to practice law. A person can fail the bar exam and still be a perfectly good lawyer, and the reverse is also true: a person can pass the bar exam and still be a lousy lawyer. The bar exam is a test of test-taking ability, but since lawyers do not take tests, no purpose is served by training them to become good test-takers.

So the bar exam does not benefit the public by ensuring rudimentary lawyering skills, and it does not benefit young lawyers by providing them with useful information. It benefits only one group of persons: existing lawyers. It does this by slowing down the entry of new lawyers into the profession, and by scaring young lawyers into cowering submissively before the awesome power of the organized bar and the licensing authorities. The whole process brings to mind *The Wizard of Oz*, in which the Tin Man and the Cowardly Lion were scared by the Great Oz until they discovered that it was just an insecure man behind a curtain. Despite all of the bombastic rhetoric about "assuring the public and the courts that lawyers are competent,"[1] the bar exam is not about competence. It is an object lesson in greed and a demonstration of how powerful interests create screening mechanisms and rites of passage to marginalize, humble, and humiliate outsiders.

The only way to pass the bar exam is to take a very expensive bar review course which reduces the law to Mickey Mouse formulae and comic book simplifications that are instantly discarded once the exam is finished. The review process thrusts students into a subterranean world of impossible outlines, study regimes, and endless gossip in search of little tricks to pass the exam. In the process, students do not pick up any practical lawyering skills and obtain zero knowledge of how to run a law practice. And since students are *expected* to pass anyway, there is little exultation in passing the exam but immense humiliation in failing, so the dangers outweigh the rewards, which is a hallmark of pointless rituals. What's worse, this expensive, intrusive, and useless ritual does not weed out a sufficient number of people to make an impact on the profession, since people who fail the exam can take it repeatedly until they pass: one California lawyer passed the bar on his forty-eighth attempt.[2] On the other hand, the bar authorities have flunked lots of people who have gone on to become highly qualified lawyers, such as Senator Hillary Clinton and Gerry Spence.[3] So the bar exam does not successfully weed out those candidates who are so incompetent that they repeatedly fail the exam, and it wrongfully excludes competent lawyers who happen to underperform on a given day. It is a total failure.

The bar exam has not been a constant phenomenon in American history. At the beginning of the twentieth century, in what is now considered the golden age of the profession, only a handful of states actually had a board of bar examiners, and only a few states required a written exam.[4] This means that many of the most esteemed lawyers in American history (for example, Justice Oliver Wendell Holmes) never took a formal bar exam of the type required nowadays. In fact, Abraham Lincoln was a bar examiner in the State of Illinois, and he once gave a bar examination and certified a young lawyer for practice in Illinois while taking a bath.[5]

The modern bar exam emerged in the second and third decades of the twentieth century as part of an effort by the WASP-influenced American Bar Association to stem the tide of new lawyers, most of them ethnic immigrants and Jews. According to one legal historian who studied the founding documents of the ABA, "The fight for higher standards was aimed in principle at incompetence, crass commercialism, and unethical behavior; but it was clear in the language of the leaders of the bar that 'the poorly-educated, ill-prepared, and morally weak candidate' meant chiefly those growing numbers of the metropolitan bars who were foreign-born, of foreign parentage, and most pointedly, Jews."[6] From the beginning, the bar examiners have communicated in code and doublespeak. They have been parading under the banner of ethics and competence, while their true purpose was simply to protect the property interests of white male lawyers.

The dominant ideology of the bar exam, as evidenced by articles in the journal *Bar Examiner* (which is basically a forum for the National Conference of Bar Examiners), portrays the state bar examiners as performing a public service by diligently adjusting the exam structure to ensure that incompetent lawyers are weeded out. That is nonsense. The bar exam has very little to do with ensuring minimal competence, and I would be extremely surprised to find more than a handful of cases in the last twenty years in which a client was protected because of knowledge that the lawyer gained while studying for the bar exam.

Competence of the type engendered by the bar exam (namely, the rote memorization of oversimplified doctrines) is basically a nonissue. Statistically speaking, clients hardly ever complain about lawyers based on *substantive* errors caused by ignorance of the law (and in any event, the bar authorities can protect clients from such errors by requiring lawyers to carry malpractice insurance). Lawyers are usually punished for *practical* errors totally unrelated to subjects tested on the bar exam, such as filing a lawsuit too late, overcharging, commingling funds, stealing a client's money, committing a crime unrelated to their law practice, or for neglect due to depression, alcoholism, or drug abuse.[7] In New York State alone, recent statistics show that more than half of all disciplinary cases involve good old-fashioned stealing of client funds, something completely unrelated to the doctrines taught on the bar exam, and something that any nonlawyer would immediately recognize as unethical.[8] This shows that the public would be better served if young lawyers were trained in the nuts and bolts of law *practice* (billing, timekeeping, recognizing psychological problems, getting help from older lawyers) than subjected to a bizarre exam in which they are taught formulaic and misleading summaries of the law that are of absolutely no help in representing a client.

The True Functions of the Bar Exam

The bar exam is not about protecting the public—it is about protecting the lawyers. It does this in two ways. First, it protects the client base of existing lawyers by limiting the number of new lawyers who might tempt away clients. Second, it beats young lawyers into passivity by making them fearful of the bar authorities, who happen to be older lawyers. Plain and simple, the bar exam is about economics and subjugation; it is a rite of passage by which the hopeful lawyer-to-be shows his willingness to do anything to please the state bar authorities in exchange for a license.

If you are looking for a parallel in literature, consider the short story by Dostoevsky entitled "A Disgraceful Affair," in which an abusive and alcoholic father tries to find someone to marry his unattractive daughter. Ultimately he finds a pathetic civil servant who is too poor to refuse. Just prior to the wedding, the abusive father forces his future son-in-law to perform a difficult dance, solely to humiliate him: "Incidentally, while there was not yet a week before the wedding, he made Pseldonymov dance the Kazatchek for him. 'That will do, I just wanted to see that you're not forgetting your place,' he said at the end of the dance."[9] That is what the bar exam is like—a pointless dance just to prove who is the boss. The bar authorities want you to remember that they control your career and your livelihood, the message being that your law license is a gift from the higher authorities and can be withdrawn at any time, so you shouldn't rock the boat too hard. Like a hazing ritual at a fraternity, the price of admission to this club is submission to a humiliating task, after which the humiliated person emerges transformed into a person who is now authorized to administer the same beating to new recruits. When this type of behavior occurs in private lives (when a battered child beats his own kids, when gang members stomp a new recruit as an initiation ceremony) it is considered a sick cycle of abuse; but somehow lawyers imbue the same process with solemnity.

Another useful literary parallel can be found in the short story entitled "The Lottery" by Shirley Jackson, which is about a small town where an innocent citizen is chosen at random each year to be sacrificed in a brutal public stoning as part of the annual harvest ritual. The story does not shock the reader with depictions of violence (indeed, the violence is only suggested at the end of the story), but rather by its depiction of how ordinary people can follow a brutal ritual blindly and without question. The social practice of public stoning had become so ingrained that when one man dared to question whether the ritual was a good idea, he was immediately silenced with an appeal to tradition: "We've always had the lottery!"[10] This is the same response that you are likely to hear when you question the bar exam.

To my mind, the bar exam performs a similar function to the lottery in Jackson's story. It is basically a rite of passage that has a mostly arbitrary relation to its stated purpose, and every year a certain number of people are singled out for failure, just like the public stoning in "The Lottery." It is a closed circle: the bar authorities cite incompetence as the justification for the bar exam, and their proof for the existence of incompetence is that so many people fail the bar exam. The exam justifies itself blindly. Reality never intrudes into the equation.

There is not a single shred of documentary evidence that the bar exam protects the public. This point must be repeated constantly: there is no proof whatsoever that the bar exam protects the public. But there is a lot of evidence that the bar exam protects older lawyers, simply by virtue of slowing down the entry of competition into the profession. Therefore, the bar exam is a "double gesture": its stated purpose (to protect the public) obscures its actual purpose. Social critic Barbara Ehrenreich made a similar point about pre-employment videos and job application tests that are becoming increasingly common in low-wage jobs: "What these tests tell employers about potential employees is hard to imagine. . . . The real function of these tests, I decide, is to convey information not to the employer but to the potential employee, and the information being conveyed is always: You will have no secrets from us."[11] Similarly, the bar exam is a symbolic performance by which the bar authorities demonstrate that they control your fate and know everything about you by virtue of your disclosures on the bar application, which are intrusive to the point of humiliation. You are only an attorney at their leisure; they give you a license and they can take it away. If you ask too many questions, you might find yourself facing a nasty investigation into your personal history.

The exam has become such a time-honored tradition ("We've always had the lottery") that it stands beyond debate, as anyone will quickly find out by suggesting that the exam be abolished. But traditions should not be followed simply because they have been around for a while. Instead, they should be critically examined, and, if necessary, discarded. As Marx said, "The tradition of all the dead generations weighs like a nightmare on the brains of the living."[12] The bar exam has become a nightmarish tradition. Looked at soberly, the bar exam accomplishes nothing except to weed out a few students who fail to study for it, and paradoxically these are often people with higher-than-average intelligence who eventually become great lawyers. Even the dumbest persons can take the exam repeatedly until they pass. In the final reckoning, only a few people get weeded out, and the reason has less to do with their incompetence to practice law than their incompetence at handling ridiculous multiple-guess exams. After all, if a person can get through an ABA-approved law school (which is a requirement for taking the bar in most states), there is good reason to suppose that the person has the ability to practice law. In any event, there is no telling who will fail the bar exam. While I was in law school (at a top-tier school), two students who were chosen as commencement speakers failed the exam.

It is a joke to believe that people who pass the exam are ready to practice. I have never met a single person who passed the bar exam and was immediately competent to represent a client. When I passed the Illinois bar, I knew the law of arson in seventeenth-century England and I knew some outdated rules for wills and trusts, but I could not tell you the structure of the Cook County court system—for example, that certain cases are to be filed in the Law Division while others are in the Municipal Division. Indeed, I vividly recall the bar review instructor telling the room full of students, "Here is a rule from the 1600s that is completely outdated nowadays but is tested on the bar exam anyway: *arson exists only when a building is torched at night, not during the day.* This is not the criminal law in Illinois, nor is it part of the Model Penal Code, but that is the law on the bar exam because they needed a general rule across jurisdictions. So make sure that you don't write down that arson occurred when a building is torched during daylight hours." In other words, to be licensed in your jurisdiction, you need to pass a test on what *isn't* the law in your jurisdiction. So I did what I was told and hit the books. I studied for hours and hours, burying myself in the bar review materials. In a sense it is incorrect to say that I was "studying," since "study" implies that the material is slowly digested, understood, and integrated into some kind of order. This is too generous a term for the bar exam review process. "Cramming" is a better term, although "rote memorization" is also appropriate.

A great amount of time in bar exam preparation is spent trying to avoid being tricked by the bar examiners. For example, students are told, "If a fact pattern has a despicable defendant who commits all sorts of offenses against a little old lady, it is probably a ruse by the bar examiners to play on your sympathy—they are trying to sucker you, so the best answer is to assume that there is some legal justification for his nasty treatment of the old lady, and you should pick the answer that lets him go." This made me wonder why the bar examiners would want to trick me with such penny-ante sleights of hand. At another point we were told, "In many cases there is no right answer, so try to pick the one that is the least wrong." How could such advice have any relevance whatsoever to the practice of law? When I wasn't trying to psych-out the bar examiners, I was busy learning an endless number of cheesy mnemonic devices and little gimmicks to make the material halfway memorable. In the end, the exam is not really about how much you know; it is about how much tedium you are willing to tolerate.

The pressure of the bar exam is almost indescribable: it generates a crippling and endless anxiety, a fear of humiliation hovering overhead like a constant black cloud. During the final weeks before the exam, many people cannot eat or sleep, and every waking moment is devoted to cramming another rule into one's head, to the point where any new thing introduced into the brain will knock another thing out. People studying for the bar exam are so self-absorbed that they cannot really have any outside relationships at the time, since one's whole being revolves around exam preparation.

When it is over, there is no feeling of mastery or happiness, just dizziness and mild regret. I can vividly recall how all of my friends agreed that we would have a huge post-exam blowout at a local nightclub where we would all get drunk and forget about the exam. Yet when we all showed up, nobody felt like partying. We were in no mood to celebrate. There was nothing to celebrate. We felt violated and used. Rather than celebrating, most students go into a three-month depression as they await the results, berating themselves endlessly for the slightest omissions on the exam. Once the results arrive, many successful candidates take immediate action by burning their bar review course materials in a cleansing ritual, which also functions as a kind of symbolic statement of protest against the entire process.

At the time that I passed the bar exam, I had never actually seen a trial from start to finish, let alone participated in one, and I had never worked on a transaction or drafted a document that had actually been signed. I had no idea what to say to a client, what to charge a client, what a retainer agreement looked like, or how to find my way around a courthouse. I felt like a doctor who had bluffed his way through medical school without learning how to take a pulse or start an intravenous line. I felt like a fraud, because I was a fraud. But I was a *licensed* fraud.

The National Multistate Exam Is neither National nor Multistate

Just as negligent parents will turn their kids over to an undisciplined babysitter, so the law schools dump their graduates in the hands of the bar review programs, the most famous of which are the BAR/BRI and PMBR programs. The baseline assumption behind these courses, sometimes covert and sometimes open, is that the bar exam is an absurd joke. There is no pretense among the bar review teachers that they are empowering students with "The Law" or generating useful skills. For example, the New York BAR/BRI runs a special session, "to dispel the madness associated with the unknowns that students face on the New York Bar Exam."[13] "Madness?" "Unknowns?" This is a frank acknowledgment that the courses are designed solely to get students to pass the exam, and that the material itself makes little or no sense and has no pedagogic function.

But there is no way around the review courses. I have never met a single person who could pass the bar after graduating from law school, because the material on the bar exam is just slightly different in content and packaging from the material taught in law school. To pass the bar it is necessary to have at your fingertips an overwhelming stockpile of one-sentence rules about miscellaneous legal subjects. These packaged rules are useless in the actual practice of law because the actual world of lawyering is ripe with ambiguity: real cases don't turn on one-sentence rules, they turn on complicated legal reasoning in which cases are analogized, distinguished, questioned, and debated. Like a disposable Styrofoam cup, the bar exam material is meant to be used once and then forgotten. The review course extends for three months of extreme boredom and memorization, turning the bar exam experience into a giant guessing game in which students consult charts and graphs to predict what subjects will be tested this year. The massive books for the bar review courses take up thousands of pages in outline form, not to mention the reams of practice exams. Even the "mini-review"—an outline of the other outlines—is hundreds of pages long. There is no attempt to tie the material together logically—it is presented as a vast knot of rules and exceptions. This review process costs in the neighborhood of $2,000.

The very existence of BAR/BRI and other review courses indicates a troubling disconnect between law school and the organized bar. Neither the law schools nor the organized bar want to be in the business of preparing students for the bar exam, so the task falls to the for-profit bar exam preparation industry. Logically speaking, it would make better sense for law schools to prepare students for the bar exam, but somehow they find this beneath themselves. Yet if the state bar authorities truly believe that the material on the bar exam is a measure of attorney competence, then they should insist that law schools teach this material so that students do not have to pay extra to learn it. As things stand, the chasm between the bar and the law schools is filled opportunistically by the review courses. This creates a bizarre cat-and-mouse game between the bar review courses and the state bar examiners, with the former always trying to predict what questions the latter will be asking on the bar exam. The state bar examiners curse the review courses for making bar passage too easy for the multitudes, while the review courses excoriate the bar examiners for unpredictability. It is a giant charade that is unworthy of the profession.

As any lawyer will acknowledge, the worst part of the bar exam is the Multistate Bar Exam (MBE), which comprises half of the bar exam in virtually all states. The MBE is a multiple-choice test that is administered uniformly across the various states and graded by a supercomputer. It is totally uniform from one state to another: the same questions are given in every state at exactly the same time under the same conditions, just like the SAT. Yet amazingly, the MBE is not transferable from state to state, unlike every other standard test ever invented (the SAT, ACT, LSAT, and GMAT, to name just a few). It turns out that only a few states will accept an MBE score from another state and then only if the test was taken in the last few years. To no one's surprise, the choice destinations (Florida, California) will not accept MBE scores from any other states.

Only lawyers could come up with such a stupid scenario. Here we have a uniform national exam, labeled the *Multistate* exam, drafted by the *National Conference of Bar Examiners*, that cannot be transferred from, say, Illinois to Florida. This means that the national Multistate exam is neither national nor multistate.

The problems with the MBE are legion. First, it is a multiple-choice exam, despite the fact that virtually no law school exams are multiple-choice. For most students, the MBE is the first multiple-choice test they have faced in at least three years; for some, it is the first multiple-choice exam since high school.

Law is not susceptible to multiple-choice exams. In law, any given fact pattern can be viewed in at least two competing but equal ways, which is precisely why the adversarial system exists. If every legal question had a single clear answer, we would not need an adversarial system of justice requiring lawyers on both sides to make competent arguments under the law. In law school, we teach law students to think through both sides of a legal conflict, but the MBE expects them to come up with a single right answer to an obscure set of facts. Further, the MBE fails to test the student's ability to construct an argument or draft an agreement; the test is totally passive, and winds up being a test of test-taking ability.

Second, the test is overwhelming and exhausting, consisting of two hundred very long multiple choice questions in a six-hour time frame. The questions on the MBE are so poorly phrased, the fact patterns so long and boring, the answers so similar, that in most cases the student narrows the choice to the two best options and makes an educated guess between them. It is no coincidence that students call the MBE a "multiple-guess" test. This explains why students emerge from the bar exam with no idea whether they passed or failed—because they narrowed the choices down to two and then guessed. In this way, a person's entire future is reduced to guesswork on a pointless exam that doesn't mirror law school or the practice of law.

Finally, the MBE questions follow a bizarre logic whereby the answers have conditionals embedded in them. For example, the correct answer to a question about the crime of arson might be, "Yes, arson was committed here, but only if the match touched the building itself." This reverses normal logic by changing an "if, then" structure into a "then, if" structure. In normal logic, premises come before a conclusion, and conditionals *precede* an answer, such as "If the match touched the wall, then there is an arson in this case." By reversing normal logic, and having long fact patterns followed by long and tortuous answers, the exam is a complete perversion of ordinary reasoning, let alone legal reasoning. I can honestly say that the exam has been totally useless to me in the years that I have practiced. Even worse, the MBE takes up half the bar exam but only tests a handful of subjects, completely avoiding important areas such as civil procedure and business law.

The MBE provides no practical skills—no drafting, no negotiating, no organization of files, no reviewing of documents; in short, nothing that lawyers actually do. One would expect that if the bar exam is a way of ensuring lawyer competence, it would mirror the concrete skills that lawyers actually use. This problem has been remedied somewhat through the adoption (in slightly more than half the states) of the Multistate Performance Test (MPT) which indeed simulates some of the legal skills that young lawyers actually use—reviewing a file, drafting a memo, preparing a motion, analyzing a regulation. But even with the MPT, the context is typically litigation-oriented and does not test for the skills used by the majority of lawyers who do not practice litigation.[14] No matter, the MBE is what students fear, for good reason. In fact, so much attention is lavished on the MBE that students rarely turn their critical gaze on the state law portion of the bar exam (consisting mostly of short essays), although this is equally blameworthy for failing to replicate the practical skills that lawyers need in everyday practice. Indeed, the essay portion often appears just as arbitrary as the MBE because the bar examiners try to hit on extremely unusual topics (cumulative voting in corporations, obscure rules of agency law, arcane miscellanea on security interests) but leave out the nuts and bolts of fundamental subjects like real estate and family law. The essay format gives the candidate more control than the MBE, but there is always a sneaking suspicion that the bar examiners are dreaming up some way to trick the candidates by introducing obtuse rules that are hidden in the fact patterns. The entire bar exam experience is an exercise in paranoia and suspicion. Instead of walking away with a sense of closure and mastery, the students walk away with a terrible feeling of having missed something that was purposely hidden from them in the first place.

Amazingly, the average raw score on the MBE is approximately 128 out of 200 for bar exams administered in July, which is equivalent to 64 percent, corresponding to the letter grade of "D" (the numbers are even lower for exams administered in February).[15] This means that the bar examiners have purposely designed an impossible test that places nearly every student on the precipice of failure. And yet when scores on the MBE started to rise in the 1990s, bar examiners were not delighted: instead, they raised the passing cut-off point to ensure that an even greater number of students would fail. The state of Ohio shifted its passing rate from 85 percent to 69 percent in a five-year period largely because it wanted to keep pace with other states;[16] Florida now fails twice as many first-time takers as it did ten years ago in order to avoid "placing the people of Florida at risk," even though there is no evidence to support such a claim;[17] and New York recently raised the passing grade on the bar exam because it was "mindful that neighboring and similar states all had higher standards."[18] In other words, students who would have been "competent" last year are now suddenly "incompetent" in the current year based on the new formula. Never mind that 95 percent of practicing lawyers would fail the bar exam if they took it tomorrow, meaning that virtually the entire practicing bar is incompetent by its own standards. In calibrating the new cutoff point, many states (including Florida and New York) are looking to a formula created by the noted bar exam expert Stephen Klein, which has been described as follows: "The heart of Klein's method uses ratings from expert panelists to estimate the percentage of passing essays on a recent administration of the state's bar exam. The process then equates the percentage of passing essays with the percentage of passing bar exams in that year. Finally, Klein determines the passing score that would have generated that percentage of passing exams—and recommends that the state adopt a score similar to that one."[19] Got that? It is just pseudoscientific mumbo jumbo for the sole purpose of limiting the number of lawyers entering the profession. The bottom line is that the exam is designed to make students believe that they have failed. In fact, the Delaware and Rhode Island bar exams allow candidates to fail five of twelve essay questions and still pass the bar; in Florida, a passing score on the Multistate Bar Exam requires answering some 60 percent of the questions correctly—an average that would lead to expulsion from law school.[20] By keeping students just on the edge of failure, the bar examiners place students in a condition of dependence and vulnerability.

In summary, then, we have an expensive, arbitrary exam that serves no discernable educational or social purpose, and is a humiliating and boring ritual of subjugation. Why, then, do so many people silently assume that the bar exam is justified in its present form? The answer is that people have been trained to accept the ideological doublespeak in which the bar exam is shrouded, namely that it protects the public by weeding out incompetent lawyers. That is precisely what the authorities would like you to believe, and they may actually believe it themselves. But nothing could be further from the truth.

The Bar Exam as Ideology

If the bar exam was truly a device for ensuring competence and weeding out subpar lawyers, then one would expect to find statistically identical pass rates across the nation. If it so happens that, say, 20 percent of law school graduates across the country are incompetent, then we should find bar passage rates of roughly 80 percent in all fifty states. This presumes that incompetent lawyers are evenly distributed across the country, which is a reasonable assumption given that most states have law schools of varying prestige (e.g., Illinois, New York, and California all have law schools in the first through fourth tiers). So logic dictates that each state will have a nearly identical distribution of incompetent candidates and, therefore, a roughly similar pass rate on the bar exam.

But it turns out that each state has a different pass rate for the bar exam, with the lowest rates in sunny states such as California (49 percent), Florida (68 percent), and Nevada (61 percent), but much higher rates in northern industrial states such as Illinois (80 percent), Indiana (74 percent), and Connecticut (78 percent).[21] To be sure, California has the highest number of unaccredited schools with low entrance requirements, which perhaps explains why the pass rate is so low, but why should Alabama have a low pass rate of 70 percent while neighboring Mississippi is 87 percent? Why is the pass rate in Utah at 92 percent while Wyoming is at 74 percent?

These numbers show once and for all that the purpose of the bar exam is *politics*, not pedagogy. It is completely ridiculous for the National Conference of Bar Examiners to suggest that 30 percent of the people who step up to the plate in Florida and Oregon lack the knowledge to practice law, while only 12 percent in Minnesota lack the same knowledge. Anyone who looks at this situation for any length of time must conclude that the bar exam is not really about competence. It is about adjusting the bar (literally!) so that it becomes a permanent obstacle for a certain number of people who would like to practice in a particular state. It acts like a funnel: it does not completely block out the competition, but slows it down. The bar authorities cannot get away with simply holding a straight-up lottery and weeding out a certain percentage of applicants, so they accomplish the same thing indirectly through the bar exam ritual.

Some states, such as Wisconsin, have the gumption to come right out and favor in-state graduates by waiving the bar exam for students who graduate from an in-state law school. If you graduate from, say, the University of Wisconsin Law School, you do not have to take a bar exam in Wisconsin. The Wisconsin Bar calls this "diploma privilege," but it is outright favoritism, pure and simple. It creates an extra barrier for out-of-state people who would otherwise like to come to Wisconsin and who expect to be on the same footing as in-state graduates when it comes to licensing requirements.

The Wisconsin system may be blatantly unjust to out-of-state law school graduates, but it is a progressive approach from the vantage point of recognizing that the bar exam is unrelated to competence to practice law. I have personally dealt with Wisconsin lawyers for over a decade because I practiced in the neighboring state of Illinois. And while nearly two-thirds of Wisconsin lawyers never took a bar exam, I have never thought to ask a Wisconsin lawyer if she took the bar exam, and the available evidence suggests that Wisconsin is in the middle of the pack with respect to the number of complaints filed against lawyers.[22] This just shows that the bar exam is not a necessary or sufficient condition for practicing law. Virtually every other state could enact a similar "diploma privilege" and nothing would be changed for the worse.

Just as I have never inquired whether a Wisconsin attorney ever passed the bar exam, I have never questioned the license of another lawyer in my home state of Illinois. Yet it so happens that I worked on several projects with an unlicensed attorney who was a partner at the large firm where I was clerking during law school. As it turns out, the partner never officially graduated from law school (he was two credits shy of graduation at Michigan Law) so he never sat for a bar exam. In other words, he had faked his way for some ten years, working up to the vaunted status of litigation partner at a leading Chicago megafirm. Ironically, his cover was blown for administrative reasons and not because of incompetence or unethical behavior. By all accounts, he was a brilliant litigator. In fact, the scandal was made public when our firm had to explain the situation in open court to a federal judge who had just awarded our firm $18,000 based on the legal work done by this nonlawyer.[23] This man's downfall and banishment from the profession had nothing to do with his ability as a lawyer. This incident shows that a person can be a great lawyer without taking a bar exam.

The bar exam is ideological because its true motivation is political, yet it parades as a public safety measure. It is also an inherently conservative institution because it freezes the status quo. This is precisely how ideology works—the true purpose of an institution is shrouded in bogus claims of necessity and inevitability. Just as slave owners once adduced "scientific" evidence that slaves were incapable of acting as full members of society, so the bar authorities trot out endless charts and graphs to justify their exams. In effect, the bar examiners have created a giant rationalization to protect the established bar, which has historically been white, male, and propertied. These people are using the bar exam to halt the entry into the profession of young law school graduates, an increasing number of whom are women and minorities.

In explaining how ideology works, Marx pointed out that unfairness and exploitation are always shrouded in some sort of legitimating system of ideas. The oppressive institution of slavery was shrouded in an ideological notion that slaves needed the guidance of Western liberators; male dominance was rationalized as a way of protecting women from their own irrationalities. With ideology, the actual motive for a belief system is kept from the view of the ideology holder: "Ideology is a process accomplished by the so-called thinker consciously, it is true, but with a false consciousness. The real motive forces impelling him remain unknown to him; otherwise it simply would not be an ideological process. Hence he imagines real or seeming motive forces."[24] This process is at work in the rationalizations that prop up the bar exam. For all the talk about protecting the public, there is little hard evidence that the bar exam provides skills that inure to the public's benefit. And there is no question that the three months of studying and anxiety engendered by the exam could be better spent in a series of pass/fail seminars in which young lawyers learned the nuts and bolts of the local court system and the fundamentals of law office management. The underlying, real purpose of the bar exam is to limit admission to the bar and to create a sense of hierarchy and submission in prospective lawyers. The existing bar exam does this exceedingly well—it weeds out a certain percentage of people and scares everybody. And it stands above criticism because anybody who dares to speak out against the bar exam is vulnerable to the accusation that he lacks standards. Given this, there is no incentive for the bar examiners to actually find a way to inculcate basic skills for prospective lawyers.

The ideological agenda of the bar examiners is clearly shown by their repeated and relentless grasping at every lame excuse to restrict the entry of new law school graduates into the profession. Over the years they have tried every cheap tactic to keep those who were not male WASPs out of the profession, often refusing to budge until the Supreme Court ruled against them. For example, bar examiners spent decades trying to exclude foreign-born lawyers from licensure, but this was stricken by the Supreme Court;[25] then states tried to keep out residents of other states, but this, too, was stricken by the Supreme Court.[26] And for a long time states tried to keep out any applicants who were members of the Communist Party, even when such persons swore under oath to follow the law.[27] State bar examiners have *never* been in the business of ensuring competence; they have *always* been in the business of preventing a free market among attorneys and keeping out undesirables (meaning anyone who looks or thinks differently).

The whole concept of each state setting up its own bar exam is completely anachronistic in the Internet age when state boundaries are increasingly meaningless. Few lawyers nowadays restrict their practice to a single state, and it is common to hear about, say, a Texas law firm representing an Arkansas corporation that is selling securities on the New York Stock Exchange through a Delaware underwriting firm and simultaneously arranging a private placement to wealthy individuals in California and Mexico. In this climate, there is something absurd about requiring a lawyer to pass the bar exam in each and every state where his clients happen to roam, or to get local counsel that will have to be brought up to speed at great time and expense. But that is precisely what states are doing, in a last-gasp effort to guarantee employment for in-state lawyers. Consider that the California Supreme Court recently sanctioned a New York firm for the unauthorized practice of law by representing a California client in a California arbitration (not requiring any court appearances).[28] The situation could get even more ridiculous if attorneys from outside the United States are allowed to counsel California clients on matters of international law under WTO and NAFTA guidelines; under these circumstances, Canadian lawyers would be allowed to come to California to make legal arguments on behalf of a California client, whereas New York lawyers would be restricted from doing the same thing.[29]

The situation is also ridiculous when it comes to reciprocal admission between two states, sometimes referred to as "admission on motion." Currently, twenty-seven states permit reciprocal admission, but only if the attorney has already practiced five to seven years in his home state—otherwise he must take the bar exam in the destination state.[30] Another ten states allow for a special "attorneys exam" consisting of essays. Still, most of the desirable states do not permit any form of reciprocity (including the highly desirable state of Florida, which presumably denies reciprocity to punish retirees). Out West, three states (Washington, Idaho, and Oregon) suddenly got the idea to allow reciprocal admission, but only among each other, excluding any other states.[31] Washington is also experimenting with a new policy of "you let us in, we'll let you in," essentially mirroring the reciprocity policy of other states. All of this playing around does not make a substantial dent in the basic postulate that lawyers are pretty well stuck in their home state, an affliction that doctors, accountants, and most other professions have found a way to avoid.

Taking an overview of this ridiculous patchwork of inconsistent and half-baked rules, one can only be struck by its complete lunacy and backwardness. There is nothing to sustain the current regime apart from the greed of established members of the bar who find themselves in the luxurious position of having all the clients, having passed the bar, and having no plans to practice law in another state. The system is great for them but terrible for young lawyers. We are presently operating under an admissions and reciprocity system that no sane person would design. Or to put the point simply, just ask yourself whether there is any rational explanation for why a twenty-five-year-old graduate of, say, Florida Coastal School of Law is deemed competent to practice law on the day that she passes the Florida bar exam, yet all nine justices of the Supreme Court would be deemed "incompetent" if they moved to Florida and hung out a shingle.

What's worse, the bar exam is only a small part of a giant unworkable system that regulates lawyers with unmatched inefficiency. Once you obtain the license, there is virtually no supervision whatsoever. Apart from one lawyer in a thousand who is weeded out on the basis of outrageous conduct, there is a small chance that a typical lawyer will be punished for wrongdoing. The statistics from Florida in the year 2000 are typical: Out of 63,000 lawyers in Florida, only 472 were subject to any form of disciplinary notice (38 disbarments, 155 sanctions, 57 public reprimands, 38 voluntary resignations, 70 admonishments, and 114 probations)[32]—hardly the iron hand of the law in a state known for merciless punishments that include the electric chair and forcing prisoners to work in striped outfits on the side of the highway. This suggests that the state bar authorities are more concerned with keeping lawyers *out* of the profession than they are with regulating the lawyers *in* the profession.

Of course, everyone agrees that the bar should have the power to weed out candidates (or licensed attorneys) who exhibit a known, established, and documented pattern of criminal or fraudulent conduct, such as repeated arrest, imprisonment, tax fraud, perjury, theft, and the like. These are the easy cases. But the bar authorities have traditionally used every excuse to weed out candidates who have done nothing wrong whatsoever, but who somehow offend the bar's sense of propriety or decorum. They are empowered to do this by having jurisdiction to pass judgment on a candidate's "good moral character" after eliciting intimate personal information.

This is how they frighten you into submission: they make you reveal every minor incident in your life, to the point where you feel so vulnerable that you just want to go home and curl up under the blankets. Statistics show that bar authorities are very likely to investigate a candidate who admits to having undergone psychiatric care (such as seeing a therapist), or is a political activist, even if the candidate has no record showing that these activities adversely affect her ability to practice. Deborah Rhode of Stanford University reviewed the statistics on revocation of licenses and concluded that "the bar's moral outrage has been largely exhausted by ceremonial inquiries and occasional outings of petty transgressors and former felons. Most garden-variety professional misconduct—incompetence, harassment, deception, and delay—is rarely reported or sanctioned."[33] Applicants are well aware that they will be called on the carpet to explain any blemishes on their record, which is why they routinely omit vital information on their bar application. In my own experience, the bar examiners in one of the states where I am licensed took the liberty of investigating every one of my friends who confessed to seeing a psychiatrist, as if this were a sign of mental instability. In fact, one candidate successfully sued the Virginia Board of Bar Examiners under the Americans with Disabilities Act based on its process of flagging applicants who confessed to having sought counseling or therapy of any kind in the past five years: "They are actually weeding out the healthiest people—the ones who are getting help," said the aspiring lawyer. It comes as no surprise that the board's expert witness could not point to a shred of evidence establishing a correlation between such mental-health questions and an inability to practice law.[34] More recently, the New Jersey bar refused to issue a license to a left-leaning young man with a history of social activism even though he passed the bar exam and was admitted to practice in neighboring New York State: his unpardonable sin consisted of traveling to Cuba three times (and returning with a few cigars) during law school, something that he disclosed in full on his bar application.[35] This case was particularly laughable since lots of law professors and lawyers have traveled to Cuba on "official" programs set up by state bar committees. It is easy to see why candidates do not trust the bar authorities.

Scared and Compliant, but Licensed at Last

The bar exam is structured such that even those who have passed with flying colors walk out of the room without any clue as to whether they passed. In a moment of candor, an honest lawyer for the New York Legal Aid

Society admitted, "I have no idea why I passed. I don't know what it measured. I spent weeks sitting on my butt memorizing stuff. Did I forget it immediately? Yes."[36] This is quite odd if you think about it. Most tests are structured so that if you study hard, you will most assuredly pass, and when you fail you at least have some idea of where you went wrong. The bar exam is not like that because the bar exam is not an ordinary test. It is a rite of passage whose entire point is simply to create the feeling of failure. This bears repeating because it is hard for most people to accept: the bar exam is designed primarily with the goal of making students believe that they have failed. That is its primary purpose: simply to make a person feel lucky to pass. This is a way of ensuring that people emerge from the exam as scared and compliant as possible. Those who pass feel that they squeaked by, so they are forever too insecure to question the wisdom of the exam.

The bar exam, like law school, draws all of its power from negative energy—not only in the sense of being a distasteful experience (which it is), but also in the sense that one is expected to pass it, so if one is successful, one has merely done what one was expected to do, whereas if one fails, there is a strong sense of humiliation. The feeling that one gets upon opening the envelope with the congratulatory letter is one of *relief*, not accomplishment. The feeling is comparable to being on a plane that lands safely in a snowstorm, or walking away from a car crash: it is not a positive experience *per se*, but rather the absence of a negative. This is how the bar examiners have set things up. Rather than inspiring students with lofty ideals, or empowering them with useful information on how to file cases or represent clients, the bar examiners subject students to an artificial black and white universe of heaven and hell, passing and failure. The bar examiners dangle this heaven/hell over the heads of the students for months on end while the exams are being graded. While one is waiting for the results from the bar examiners, one curses them and the very idea of a bar exam. Yet when one passes the exam, all is forgiven—one has joined the other side. From that vantage point, it almost seems reasonable to demand that the next generation go through the same process, because "I went through it."

After passing the bar and practicing law for more than a decade, I can recall only one or two incidents when the bar review materials came to mind. All the rest of it was a complete waste of time. Like most lawyers, I got the license, put the certificate on the wall, took mild enjoyment in having passed, and then tried to forget the entire experience. I could say that my experience was bad, but not as bad as having to take the same exam again, which several of my friends had to do. They all eventually passed, and none of them ever had any idea why they failed the first exam and passed the second. Suddenly, somehow, they became "competent" to practice law in Illinois.

The bar exam should be replaced with a series of seminars and practical courses in the nuts and bolts of law firm practice, litigation, and transactional work. During the three-month period now reserved for the bar review course, students could learn basic skills that are missing on the present bar exam, such as the ability to meet with a client and draft a retainer agreement; the ability to formulate a bill to a client along with a memorandum on the status of the matter; the capacity to write a complaint, motion, and pretrial brief; the capacity to form business entities and trusts; the ability to draft a will, and a separation agreement; and knowledge of the local rules for the proper formatting of complaints, cover sheets, fees, appearances, and so forth. These seminars could be skills-based and graded on a pass/fail basis, such that students could retake the seminar every month until they passed, much like the driving license test.

Alternatively, the bar exam could be replaced with a mandatory apprenticeship requirement that assigned law school graduates to practitioners for a six-month period, during which time they would acquire the skills listed above. The supervising lawyer could then sign an affidavit attesting that the young lawyer performed representative skills sufficient to practice law on her own. The apprenticeship could even be arranged with public interest firms of the apprentice lawyer's choosing, which would be a good way to encourage pro bono work among lawyers. A variation of this approach (one that would allow students who elected public service to opt out of the Multistate Bar Exam) was recently proposed in New York State, but the organized bar responded by raising the passing score on the traditional bar exam in order to "protect the public."[37]

Another possibility is to transform the final semester of law school into an extended bar exam preparatory course. This would leave the bar exam intact, but it would at least save thousands of dollars that each student now pays to the bar review courses.

A final alternative is to simply abolish the bar exam and let law school graduates go straight into practice in the state where they obtained their law degree. This would be preferable to the current arrangement, since three months spent in the actual practice of law would be more useful to a recent graduate than three months of cramming, memorization, and anxiety.

The idea of abolishing the bar exam sounds radical. But it isn't radical from a historical perspective, since the modern bar exam is a relatively recent invention.

And if we do nothing, we simply affirm and ennoble the existing injustice of the current arrangement, which is a complete joke.

chapter four:
The *Structure* of
Law Firm Practice:
Alienated
"Associates"

It is nearly impossible for a new attorney to open a law office. First, a young lawyer does not obtain the skills for practicing law while in law school, so she would be committing malpractice left and right if she opened a law office. Second, the market for clients is extremely competitive, and in any event, clients are hesitant to hire a young attorney. And finally there is the question of money. According to figures from a study by the American Bar Association, a young lawyer in a solo practice generates $60,000 in annual expenses (including rent, equipment, secretarial services, library costs, bar association fees, advertising, and insurance) before the lawyer generates a dime of profit.[1] This means that "hanging out a shingle" is not an option for law school graduates, especially those who need cash immediately to pay down their student loans.

Virtually without exception, a lawyer fresh out of school has no choice but to seek employment with a private law firm, if such a job can be found. So every year, tens of thousands of law school graduates pin their hopes on landing a position as an "associate" at a law firm. As this chapter will indicate, that position is no picnic. While law students are often courted by law firms with extravagant promises about the possibility of maintaining a reasonable lifestyle, the naked truth is that law firms have an overwhelming interest in working young lawyers to death. One young lawyer realized this after his first year at a big firm: "I found that most of my colleagues and friends in other top firms were having similar doubts about their careers. Our firms seemed to differ in name only; as associates, we were fungible commodities no matter where we worked."[2] This cycle of longing and disappointment begs for an explanation: Why do so many law students desperately want to be associates, yet become so depressed and alienated once they get the sought-after position? How can so many educated and otherwise cynical people be so deluded about what awaits them? And if they know what awaits them, why do they still march forward?

The cycle of expectation and regret is explained to some degree by the ignorance of law students about what really goes on in the legal profession, combined with the ability of law firms to conceal the truth about what happens behind closed doors. There is a tremendous amount of bluffing, posturing, selective amnesia, and downright misrepresentation on both sides in what can only be described as a *courtship* between firms and law students (I use this word intentionally because the relationship includes dressing up, lavish dinners, exchange of gifts and notes, public announcements, and other rituals more appropriate to an engagement than to recruitment of employees). Law students are in dire need of high-paying positions, and they are desperate to feel wanted by members of the legal profession, since the only lawyers they met in law school (namely their professors) were punitive and distant. At the same time, law firms are desperate for young lawyers to generate billable hours that translate into profits for the partners, so there is an incentive for the law firms to say anything in order to hook the students into accepting positions. A relationship of this kind—born of dependence and cemented with lies—will always turn out to be disappointing.

Law students make a big production out of choosing Firm X over Firm Y, and the firms do their part to perpetuate the conceit that each firm is unique, but the bottom line is the same for young lawyers at every firm: associates are put into high-pressure positions where advancement is based on billable hours, and where partnership is conditioned on bringing new clients to the firm. Nowadays, merely being a good lawyer is not enough; one must also be a self-sustaining profit-center, or attached umbilically to a lawyer who fits this description. This is a lot of pressure. Not only must the young lawyer work exorbitant hours and give up her personal life, but also she must simultaneously develop a specialty and attract major business to the firm. These pressures create a shocking rate of attrition. For example, I joined a big firm along with twenty-five other law school graduates from top schools, but after five years only a handful of us remained with the firm. Most of these people shifted jobs several times, always searching in vain for the one firm willing to buck the trend of overwork and attrition. Looking back, our biggest mistake was to view law firms as if they were different from any other moneymaking enterprise.

Although most law firms are technically partnerships, they are essentially no different from profit-driven corporations, where the owners (in this case, partners) have interests antagonistic to the workers (the associates). The legal profession is moving away from the almost medieval *guild* quality that it once retained, and is moving toward the *factory* model that dominates our industrial society.[3] The legal system now has two *classes*, and so to understand what is happening in the profession, we must go back to Karl Marx's notion of class struggle. Amazingly, Marx predicted—a century and a half ago—that professions would be turned into businesses: "[Capitalism] has stripped of its halo every occupation hitherto honored and looked up to with reverent awe. It has converted the physician, *the lawyer*, the priest, the poet, the man of science into its paid wage laborers."[4] The transformation of the legal profession into a business (complete with advertising and public relations) has cheapened the profession and turned law firms into commodity-producing factories that churn out legal services in the same way that factories churn out widgets. In fact, I recently asked a friend what type of law his firm specialized in; he told me, "We produce widgets." I instantly knew what he meant, namely that the content of what they produced was irrelevant since nobody at the firm cared about it anyway.

In most law firms nowadays, the young lawyer is a mere entry on a ledger, an hourly wage-slave trying to compete in a scarce economy, with every move being monitored by law firm administrators in much the same way that telemarketers are forced to make a certain number of calls per hour while the supervisor listens.

There has always been a business dimension to the legal profession, for the simple reason that lawyers brought in fees, paid expenses, and distributed profits just the same as any other business. But something always prevented law from dissolving into a mere business enterprise. For one thing, unlike businessmen who self-consciously adopt hardball tactics in the open market-place, lawyers take an oath to uphold justice as "officers of the court" and "administrators of justice," which means that there is a public dimension to their calling. And law was always considered a learned profession that was, on the surface at least, driven by intellectual rigor at the same time that it offered a comfortable lifestyle. In fact, the Illinois Rules of Professional Conduct still give voice to the public duty to represent citizens at the least cost:

> The practice of law is a public trust. Lawyers are the trustees of the system by which citizens resolve disputes among themselves, punish and deter crime, and determine their relative rights and responsibilities toward each other and the government. . . . Legal services are not a commodity. Rather, they are the result of the efforts, training, judgment, and experience of the members of a learned profession. . . . [I]t is the duty of all lawyers to seek resolution of all disputes at the least cost in time, expense and trauma to all parties and to the courts.[5]

This is enshrined in Illinois law (and in most states) but it sounds almost anachronistic in an age when a single law firm can generate annual revenue in excess of $1 billion,[6] when a law firm can be accused of overbilling a client for $57 million,[7] when the best-known law firms represent *institutions* instead of people, and when lawyers publicly boast about their skill in delaying cases and outspending opponents.[8]

Clearly, the logic of the capitalist system has invaded and overtaken the profession, ushering in sweeping changes in the way that lawyers practice law and in how they think about themselves. I believe that Marxist theory, with its subtle insights into capitalist society, best captures the mechanism at work in the transformation of the law from a profession into a business, and I believe that Marx's concept of "alienated labor" best captures the prevailing mood among young lawyers.[9]

Much of the unhappiness among young lawyers is directly traceable to the *structural features* of law firms, wholly apart from the specific legal tasks that lawyers are given. By *structural features* I mean the environmental forces weighing on the young lawyer: the compensation scheme, the promotion guidelines, the chain of command, the division of labor, and the general pyramid structure of the entire enterprise. Accordingly, this chapter deals with unhappiness attributable to the *structural,* or environmental, features of law practice. The next chapter treats the *content* side of the practice, including the unsavory, boring, and unethical legal tasks demanded of young lawyers. For now, I want to demonstrate that the structural framework at most law firms is guaranteed to produce misery in young lawyers.

Associate = Wage-Slave Employed at Will

A law firm will hire a young lawyer only if he can generate surplus value in an amount necessary to reproduce both himself (as a worker) and to reproduce his bosses (in the lifestyle to which they have become accustomed). If a young lawyer is billing 2,000 hours at the rate of $150/hour, then she is generating $300,000, which covers salary and overhead (say, $200,000), with the surplus (say, $100,000) to be shared by the partners. The formula is blood simple. The more attorneys in the firm, the more profit. To feed this machine, the firm needs sufficient clients to keep the young lawyers busy. This problem is solved by refusing to grant full partnership to a young lawyer unless he can attract new clients (seduced away from other lawyers, no doubt). Like a shark that must keep swimming to avoid sinking, the present-day law firm is caught in an escalating cycle of higher salaries and more billable hours, constantly hunting for new clients and standing ready to eliminate young lawyers if necessary. This structure creates an *inversion* of priorities. Instead of being a professional firm that happens to make money, the modern law firm is a money-making firm that happens to involve a profession.

World-famous trial lawyer Gerry Spence has pointed out that the basic structure of a law firm is no different from a house of ill repute, a message that he delivered to a Stanford law student who sought advice on whether to join a large firm. As Spence told the law student,

> The firm will bill your time out at a hundred and fifty an hour or more, and you'll make them a lot of money, like the sale of any commodity at a profit. It's sort of like the women they used to run up in the whorehouse in Laramie when I was a kid. They charged five dollars a trick. They got to keep half and the madam got half. The more women the madam had working for her, the more she made. The prettier they were, the better the madam's business, and you're as pretty as they come—"the best and the brightest," as they say. And if you work long enough and hard enough, someday you may even become a madam yourself.[10]

But law firms have always differed from whorehouses in two key respects. First, lawyers are not free to do anything that a client asks—they are bound by rules of professional conduct. Second, it was considered undignified for lawyers to publicly proclaim how much money they were making. For most of the twentieth century, the two constraints (ethics and propriety) were successful in preventing the profession from devolving into a business. Lawyers were not supposed to be motivated solely by money, but rather by professionalism, and this kept them from seeing everything through the lens of dollars and cents. But that is no longer the case, and law firms now boast openly about their profits, just like any other business.

The rules of professional conduct have been useless in stopping the pervasive greed within the profession. Recent evidence from the savings and loan fiasco in the 1990s and the Enron debacle of 2001 suggests that law firms will skirt ethical issues in exchange for high fees, judging from their willingness to set up fraudulent Ponzi schemes and houses-of-cards. The recent tobacco settlements indicate that lawyers are happy to use Rambo-style tactics to scare plaintiffs and delay lawsuits for decades. As things stand, most lawyers at large firms will not *break* an ethical rule outright, but when the money is flowing they have proven quite willing to *bend* the rules.

There was a time when the underlying economics of law firms was a private matter. But in the 1980s, trade magazines began to publish figures on the profitability of each law firm, culminating in the *American Lawyer's* annual full-color glossy centerfold (there is no other way to describe it) depicting the one hundred most profitable law firms in America. As profitability was made public, young lawyers started demanding higher salaries, and law firms started to combine and grow exponentially. But partners would not give away their money to new associates via higher salaries unless they could make it up on the back end by having the associates work longer hours. By the 1990s, the profession had become a business, and a sick cycle had been created—greedy law students were demanding higher salaries, so law firms were demanding higher billable hours to pay these salaries, while law school tuition went upward in light of how much students would earn when they graduated.

On the surface, law firms do not look like businesses. But make no mistake, law firms are run like businesses in that they value profitability over collegiality, efficiency over innovation, and competition over cooperation. While most law firms have a party line about collegiality between partners and associates, the relationship is more accurately described as one of economic parasitism and high burnout and attrition. There is a good reason that young lawyers often refer to their firms as "sweatshops." The prevailing posture of the legal profession was well captured in a recent statement by a retired judge: "Efficiency has become a priority while the mentoring and personalized training of associates has almost vanished. . . . There is a growing feeling that the profession has become tilted toward the commercial, rather than the service, component."[11] Clearly, lawyers have become divided into two classes.[12] The first class owns an equity stake in a law practice and has a loyal and portable client base. These lawyers are the functional equivalent to the "legal bourgeoisie," since by possessing the client base they control the source for the legal work to be done by other lawyers.[13] The second class consists of young lawyers who lack both an equity stake in a firm and a portable client base. The members of this class have nothing to offer except their labor power: they are the functional equivalent of the "legal proletariat." Whereas the profession was once modeled on a stairway that a young associate could climb to reach partnership, the profession is now modeled on a treadmill where young lawyers often run in place forever without advancing.

The typical law firm is structured as a partnership. The "equity partners" share the net profits; below them are the "junior partners" who are paid straight salary but stand in line to become equity partners; at the bottom of the pyramid are the "associates" who are paid a straight salary and are expected to generate a certain number of billable hours. The required billable hours have shot up dramatically over the past twenty years, such that young attorneys are now required to bill hundreds of hours more than their mentors were required to bill. As a partner at a large firm recently put it, "I don't think that anyone would feel that they were at the top of their class unless they were billing at least 2,000 hours a year. As advancement toward partnership has become more competitive, people feel that doing the bare minimum is not sufficient for continued success. And the reality is, that's true."[14] By way of comparison, a Harvard graduate in 1965 (e.g., someone who is sixty-four years old today) was expected to bill 1,600 hours per year while working at a big firm in Boston or New York;[15] the figure was slightly lower for Atlanta and midwestern cities.[16] The difference between 1,600 hours and 2,100 hours is decisive: it represents 15 to 20 extra billable hours per week—two full extra days that a lawyer has to work. A young attorney who wrote a book called *Double Billing* described how billing 2,000 hours affected his life:

> To bill 2000 hours, which is common among big-firm associates, I routinely worked 11-hour days and at least one weekend day, and often worked past midnight and through the weekend. Dinner was eaten from a plastic tin in a conference room. Home was an office down the hall. And I wasn't unduly masochistic. Many associates bill 2500 hours, 3000 hours, and more. No wonder job satisfaction among lawyers is so low. . . . While it's difficult to sympathize with 'exploited' workers who make six-figure salaries, there's a reminder here for the rest of us: Money does not buy job satisfaction. Indeed, in the case of corporate lawyers, it buys the opposite.[17]

Even Justice Rehnquist of the United States Supreme Court expressed concern that the requirement to bill 2,000 hours would "sharply curtail the productive expenditure of energy outside of work," and would create "temptations to exaggerate the hours actually put in."[18]

This obsession with billable hours is curious when we consider that billing by the hour is relatively new, having emerged as the preeminent method of billing in the last quarter century. Prior to that time, most firms used fixed rates that were quoted in advance. This practice was encouraged by local bar associations, which often published minimum rates that lawyers could not underbill. In the 1970s, the Supreme Court struck minimum fee schedules as anticompetitive and also permitted lawyer advertising, setting the stage for a heightened awareness of fees, competition, and self-promotion. As the Court conceded in the 1970s, "[T]he belief that lawyers are somehow 'above' trade has become an anachronism."[19] At first, lawyers resisted billing by the hour because it required such an arduous process of record keeping. But lawyers eventually realized that hourly billing was a bonanza. True, it took away the *floor* for what a lawyer could charge (by abolishing the minimum fee schedules), but it also removed the *ceiling*. As long as a law firm could produce a record showing that the time was spent on legal matters, the bill was bona fide and had to be paid by the client. And so the practice became widespread, not because everyone acknowledged that it was the best way to practice law or to bill clients, but for reasons of historical accident.[20]

What this means is that billing by the hour is not natural, essential, or necessary. It is not built into the fabric of lawyering. It is a recent experiment that can be reversed if a sufficient number of lawyers are willing to put it to an end. Unfortunately, billing by the hour remains dominant in the industry and will likely remain so. Recent surveys indicate that large law firms rely on it for over 90 percent of matters that they handle.[21] This remains true even though the president of the American Bar Association has called upon lawyers to explore alternative methods.[22]

Billing by the hour creates a sharp dichotomy of interests within a given firm. The partners have the clients, but they need the younger lawyers for labor power; the young lawyers have the labor power but do not have any clients. Each group needs the other but is hostile about the fact that it is dependent on the other group, and hence a weird kind of master-slave dialectic is at work in most firms, with the senior lawyers complaining in private about the greedy and lazy young associates, and the young associates complaining about the stodgy and secretive partners. Despite the pretense of collegiality among partners and associates, the two groups represent entirely different social strata.

Since job security and continued employment are based on the extent of one's client base, the older attorneys hold onto their power by retaining a group of jealously guarded clients, whereas younger attorneys have few clients and are therefore in a perpetual state of dependence on the older attorneys. In effect, this creates a sort of firm within a firm, where the older lawyers farm out their work to certain associates (thereby "hiring" the associate), and these associates rack up billable hours (and goodwill) by pleasing certain partners. Eventually, so the story goes, the associate will "make partner," that is, she will become first a partner in name only and will soon advance to the status of "equity partner." The basic idea is that the older lawyers provide the young lawyers with training, clients, and the possibility for a share in the profits, whereas the young lawyers provide the firm with labor power. Ideally, this system functions as an apprenticeship in which the young lawyer advances to the status held by the older lawyers, and then continues this tradition by training a new crop of associates.

The general consensus is that this system worked for quite a while, in that the young lawyers gradually attracted clients of their own, or took over clients from retiring partners, and then took on a new class of apprentices to begin the cycle anew. Young lawyers saw older lawyers as mentors, and they really felt that they could advance with a reasonable amount of effort. And even if a lawyer was socially inept but intellectually sound, he would be kept around and would eventually be given partnership or a steady income. But over the past two decades a malaise has developed, and part of this malaise is due to the way in which young attorneys have come to be treated by older attorneys. Young lawyers have begun to think of themselves less as professionals and more as ordinary wage workers. Law firms have become increasingly like factories, as the focus has shifted to a concern with the bottom line. For the first time in American history, law firms have grown to gigantic size and are now managed by nonlawyer accountants, marketing directors, and administrators who spend their days reviewing spreadsheets on the productivity of individual worker bees. In this shift from a professional paradigm to a business paradigm, young lawyers are rarely mentored in the classic sense because mentoring takes time and detracts from billable hours.[23] In any event, many partners see no point in mentoring, since there is little likelihood that the mentored attorney will stay on to become a partner in the firm. Because of these changes, the apprenticeship model no longer fits the way in which the legal profession operates because it fails to capture the fears, anxiety, and competition felt by young lawyers. In terms of job security, competition, and likelihood of advancement, most lawyers have more in common with law firm secretaries than they do with partners.

In any event, the traditional path from associate to partner is no longer secure. As *Business Week* reported, "partnership" is not what it used to be because "partner" is no longer synonymous with "owner": "Lawyers can no longer count on a glittering partnership as a reward for years of toil. Many now find that they are little more than career employees, even when they win the vaunted title [partner]."[24] In fact, the position of *associate* is no longer secure, because law firms have begun to do something that was long considered taboo, namely to lay off attorneys. Surely something strange is afoot when "associates" are employed at will, and "partners" don't share in the partnership income. This suggests that these labels disguise the true relationships here. For the sake of honesty, we should drop all the references to "associates" and "partners" and simply tell it like it is—a few men at the top own it all, and the rest are merely workers.

At present, no young attorney can feel safe. Job security is not guaranteed by adequate job performance. An attorney needs to be more than competent; she needs a loyal and secure group of clients that would follow wherever she went, namely "portables" or a "book of business." But winning clients is not easy. Merely providing adequate representation within the bounds of the law is not enough: one has to be willing to do *anything* for the client. And even when one gets a client, there is always a looming suspicion that the client can be seduced away by another lawyer. As competition for clients increases, partners begin to guard their clients jealously, often issuing strict instructions that other attorneys are not to speak with their clients (in fact, I have been chewed out for calling a client to ask a simple question without getting the prior approval of the managing partner). Within law firms, the once uniform class of partners begins to divide into two classes: rainmakers (those who brought clients into the firm) and nonrainmakers (partners who were given an equity stake prior to the requirement that partners bring clients into the firm). For practical purposes, there is no unified "firm" any longer, since that entity fragments into conflicting factions, with resentments and mutual recriminations flying in every direction. In place of team spirit, there arises a star system in which a neverending supply of obsequious junior partners and associates struggles vainly to placate the rainmakers and to align themselves with the heroes of the hour.

A recent article in *American Lawyer* referred to the structure of law firms as a "veil of tiers" after noting that 75 percent of the top firms are moving lawyers to the nonequity partnership track (up from 55 percent ten years ago).[25] Even this pro-business magazine that functions as a tabloid for big firms was forced to conclude in Marxist fashion that "those wonderful profits per partner are coming, in the aggregate, at the expense of partners who aren't truly owners of the firm."[26] In the face of the difficulty of making partner in the first place, let alone earning full equity status, a growing number of young lawyers are simply leaving law firms without even trying. A recent study by the National Association for Law Placement found that young associates are "leaving law firms in droves before they can even be considered for partner" because the brass ring appears unattainable and ultimately undesirable.[27] In other words, it becomes a system of mutual exploitation: the young lawyers are using the firms to gain a few years of experience but have no sense of loyalty or moral commitment to the firm, while the partners have good reason to overload and ignore the young lawyers. The most laudable aspects of a professional relationship—mentoring, loyalty, trust, advancement—fall by the wayside in the face of economic pressures.

And when partners at law firms get really greedy, they can always cannibalize themselves, as occurred recently when the Sidley Austin law firm demoted thirty-five partners despite having a banner year, thereby prompting the Equal Employment Opportunity Commission to investigate on the basis of age discrimination because so many of the demoted partners were over the age of fifty-five.[28] The incident illustrates how greed eclipses collegiality in the modern law firm. Some law firms are completely overt about the practice of forcing out partners who don't bring in enough business. When this happened at megafirm Rogers & Wells, a partner said, "You're either a rainmaker or a potential rainmaker, or you're out the door."[29]

In addition to the competition *between* firms for a limited number of clients, there emerges competition *within* firms for the privilege of working under certain high-profile rainmaking partners. The attorneys in a given firm are no longer bound together in competition against outside firms; instead, each attorney is engaged in an intrafirm conflict with her officemates as they compete for a limited number of partnership spots. Lawyers become hyper-paranoid, worried about a thousand things that can derail their career: losing a case, competition within the firm, an economic downturn, the inability to generate a client base, bad blood within the firm. In this climate, lawyers can ill afford to be worried about the social mission of the profession, with the result that pro bono commitments have shrunk to as low as thirty minutes per week.[30] To be sure, bickering and office politics can be found in any office, but they take on an unparalleled intensity and frequency in law firms. After all, we are talking about *lawyers*.

The most recent trend in the legal profession is the breaking apart and merging of giant law firms, a phenomenon that brings together hundreds of lawyers who have nothing personal in common. As a result, the only thing holding the members of a law firm together is the quest for more money. As law professor Patrick Schiltz points out, "The bigger a firm is, the harder it is for its members to agree on anything other than money . . . so it becomes the only currency at big firms."[31] When money is the central focus, lawyers stop caring about the law anymore. As one observer put it, "The 80s were a bizarre time and the changes from that time have become endemic now. Law firms today would manufacture widgets if they could make a profit on them."[32] This should be obvious from the revelation that law firms were adding 40 percent mark-ups to faxes, phone calls, and even breakfast served to clients.[33] But more broadly, law firms are trying to get rich by morphing into gigantic one-stop multidisciplinary firms that offer accounting, title reporting, and business consulting on top of legal representation. In fact, accounting giant Ernst & Young has recently "aligned" itself with a new law firm, so the name "Ernst & Young" appears in the name of the firm.[34] It is a wonder that law firms don't sell coffee and doughnuts on the side to make a few bucks.

From the minute they leave law school, young lawyers face a minefield of problems. First, they must compete against hordes of other lawyers to get that all-important first job, and to accomplish this goal they often take jobs with firms that offer little or no possibility for advancement. The job search puts them in competition with their classmates, not only in a free-floating generalized competition among a class of recent graduates, but in a specific struggle against their friends for particular jobs. And once a job is actually obtained, the constant pressure of producing in order to avoid being laid off results in working long hours to please the partners and to prove oneself more profitable than other associates. Further, since there is a severe pressure to win every case in order to generate income and keep clients, younger attorneys find themselves in excessive competition with opposing counsel in every case and transaction. And finally, associates are competing directly with partners in order to attract clients, with each attorney trying to secure a book of business. As one might expect, all of this competition and job insecurity comes at a heavy price.

The equity owners of a law firm, as a class, are similar to factory owners and corporate CEOs. The only distinguishing feature is that a law partner refers to his subordinates as *associates* while the factory owner usually calls his workers by their real name, *employees*. Although the general public tends to see all lawyers as members of a united class (since they are all members of the same profession), the truth is that this class is deeply divided into owners and workers. This is why we need to get rid of the label *associate*. It wrongly obscures the attorney's true status as a worker. It creates the false impression that the attorney is *associated* with the owners of the firm (whatever that means), when in fact the vast majority of young lawyers are employed at will and can be fired for any reason. The term *associate* is a so-called *survival*, a legal relic similar to terms like *dower* and *fee tail*. Terms like *associate* and *of counsel* have no real meaning or use beyond obscuring the true roles played by lawyers. If you have any doubts about this, consider that Wal-Mart insists on calling its workers "associates," even though a huge percentage of them are paid minimum wage, with no health benefits, forced to rely on food stamps and government assistance to survive.[35] And yet associates are not even the bottom of the legal barrel, a distinction that belongs to contract lawyers who perform the real scut work for an hourly wage. In fact, a group of contract lawyers recently sued a big firm under the Fair Labor Standards Act even though that law doesn't apply to *attorneys*, under the theory that the "monkey work" they were performing was so routine that it did not constitute the practice of law.[36]

To make things worse, attorneys are bombarded with images of lawyers that do not resonate with their experiences. Television shows such as *Matlock*, *JAG*, and *Law and Order* (and to a lesser extent, *The Practice*) depict confident, established lawyers who find personal fulfillment in the law, have the autonomy to choose their cases, enjoy the luxury of extensive client contact, take pride in their legal work, and serve the community. These programs can seem downright absurd and cruel to young lawyers who see their jobs as rote and boring, and who lack autonomous control of their work project. Lawyers are confronted with a gap between their self-image and the image offered in the media. The disjunction between social expectation and bitter reality makes the young lawyer only more confused and alienated.

I have already hinted at the Marxist view of the legal profession when I noted that the bar is divided into two classes, owners and workers. There is also a Marxist backdrop to my claim that the increasing "capitalization" of the legal profession is removing the last vestiges of the guildlike elements of the profession. But now I want to go further and explain how Marx's concept of alienation is an excellent model for capturing the feelings of estrangement among young lawyers. Put simply, there has been a shift in the relations of production from a cooperative system of work (modeled on the guild and apprenticeship) to a wage-based system (modeled on the factory). Law firms have become factories and legal services have become commoditized. This structural change in the way law is practiced creates elevated levels of un-happiness and disillusionment among young lawyers.

Marx and the Four Types of Alienation

In a profit-driven system, the worker finds himself exploited (and alien-ated) in four distinct ways.[37] First, there is alienation from the physical prod-uct of one's labor. Second, there is alienation from one's productive power. Third, there is alienation from one's essence, or "species being." And finally, there is alienation from other people. I will discuss these in turn, and after explaining each type of alienation, I will discuss how it manifests itself in the experiences of young lawyers.

The *first* type of alienation discussed by Marx is alienation from the ob-jects of one's production. In a capitalist economy where workers lack mean-ingful control of a business enterprise, the worker is told what to produce and when to produce, and he produces the object for another person, at the con-trol of another person. Marx summarizes this experience:

> The object which labor produces—labor's product—confronts [man] as something alien, as a power independent of the producer. . . . The worker is related to the product of his labor as to an alien object. . . . [T]he life which he has conferred on the object confronts him as something hostile and alien.[38]

This type of alienation can be illustrated by the experience of an assembly-line worker (say, a person who installs hinges on car doors), who does not own stock in her company and has no ability to dictate what she makes, how she makes it, or the conditions under which it is made. The worker is con-fronted by the finished product (say, an expensive car) as if it were something apart from her labor that helped create it. Of course, the worker can switch jobs in order to produce a different product (say, computer chips instead of door hinges), but the worker herself lacks the means to dictate what she makes and what becomes of the product. And in a tough economy, she must take whatever work comes her way, which means that she may end up mak-ing pillows or bombs or burritos—the choice is not up to her.

This type of alienation is particularly endemic among young lawyers who need a job, any job, and have to resign themselves to providing whatever services the market requires. The young lawyer may want to help the poor, but because of the market she will most likely *sue* the poor. This type of alien-ation is also very common in lawyers assigned to work on small aspects of big projects. Without being informed of the overall project, the young lawyer feels like an errand boy assigned to random tasks. Some of the most alienating tasks include blue-sky work (looking up the securities law of fifty states) and due diligence (poring over reams of documents in search of something potentially damaging). Other mundane tasks involve appearing for routine court calls on cases for which the partners take credit, or cite-checking on legal briefs. In each of these cases, the young lawyer performs work which is unrecognized by the client, and there is no possibility for a genuine intellectual engagement with the work itself, which is repetitive, boring, and removed from actual human contact. The lawyer does not see herself in her work, does not realize herself in what she does. She performs tasks that would be done by machine if it were at all possible. On these tasks the lawyer is a billing robot that generates profit for someone else. The lawyer may see a portion of her work incorporated into the final product given to the client (e.g., in the final court documents or in the transaction binder after the deal closes) but she does not see it as *her* work. Like an assembly-line worker who welds rivets to car doors for ten hours every day, she has no relationship with the ultimate consumer, nor does she have control of her own production.

Because there is so little contact with actual human clients (indeed, the client is often an impersonal corporation looming in the distance), the young lawyer gets the impression that she is not working for an actual client, but is laboring for the partners and senior associates. It is as if she is twice removed from the real world—the client hires the senior partner, who in turn hires a younger partner, who in turns gives the nod to the younger associate. In the process the profession loses its social meaning for the young lawyer. Not only does the young lawyer's work lack a connection to the community at large, but the lawyer herself lacks any connection outside the firm. What gets lost in the process is the social meaning of the law as a helping profession. The lawyer's labor power, which is essentially a social attribute for the betterment of society, becomes a means for making money. The inner world of the lawyer—locked in his room, surrounded by reams of documents, his face glued to the computer screen—closes in upon itself, and the lawyer forgets that he is situated in a real world of real people with real needs.

At many law firms and corporations, there is a widely held but mistaken impression that stress and overwork are inevitable. None of the partners will assume responsibility for the excessive demands of the profession. A partner might concede that if it were up to him, things would be structured differently (say, to promote meaningful work and justice by lowering salaries and raising the pro bono commitment), but things are not up to him: after all, the client must be zealously represented. All too often, partners pass the buck by going along with a dehumanizing and stultifying law firm structure, on the theory that they are powerless to redirect the priorities of "The Firm." In existential parlance, this move is known as "bad faith," the idea that one is compelled to act a certain way, just as a rock is compelled to fall according to gravity. By this way of thinking, the lawyer reconciles himself to the existing arrangement and the values perpetuated by it. The lawyer may recognize in private that his client (a corporation) is acting dubiously in laying off thousands of workers so insiders can get rich, but he will insist that it is not *he* who is doing it, but rather the client, or the firm, or the market, or society as a whole. The system becomes its own justification, and no one is responsible for anything.

The *second* type of alienation discussed by Marx is alienation from one's productive power. For Marx, the self is realized in free, creative, spontaneous production. But under capitalism, the worker sells his productive power as if it were an object, thereby alienating part of his humanity:

> But the exercise of labor power, labor, is the worker's own life-activity, the manifestation of his own life. And this life-activity he sells to another person in order to secure the necessary means of subsistence. Thus his life activity is for him only a means to enable him to exist. He works in order to live. He does not even reckon labor as part of his life, it is rather a sacrifice of his life.[39]

Marx's description of the worker captures the sentiments of most lawyers that I have met in private practice: "[I]n his work, therefore, he does not affirm himself but denies himself, does not feel content but unhappy. . . . The worker therefore only feels himself outside his work, and in his work he feels outside himself. His labor is not the satisfaction of a need; it is merely a means to satisfy needs external to it."[40] In other words, what the worker produces is first and foremost *wages* so that he can subsist: having given up hope for finding his meaning in the act of *production*, he waits for work to be over so that he can realize himself in the *consumption* and accumulation of objects. And this is why so many lawyers have what sociologist David Reisman once called an "objectless craving" to fill the void with new acquisitions.

The alienation from one's productive power affects young lawyers in several ways, but it is hammered home by the requirement that they keep track of every movement so that billable time is maximized. Anyone who has contact with lawyers will testify that they have a rather odd notion of time, such that they see time itself as if it were divided up in quarter-hour units. As one lawyer who recently left the profession put it: "I felt like Pigpen [from the *Peanuts* comic strip], with a cloud of dirt over my head. But my cloud was billable hours. No matter what I did, I felt like I should be in the office doing work, not doing specific client work but racking up hours. I started to believe that I wasn't good because I didn't bill enough hours, even though the clients would compliment me for getting things done."[41] Notice how this attorney's self-assessment was tied to the number of hours she worked, not to the fact that clients praised her work, nor even the substance of the work that she was doing.

Most firms now have an electronic billing system that lets attorneys log their time directly into the computer system, allowing the attorney to pull up his entire daily, weekly, or yearly billable hours, complete with a summary of the dollar value of his work. This low-cost software allows the firm to track each lawyer as if he were a private profit center. With a few strokes on a keyboard, a manager can see how many hours an associate has billed, the cash value of the billable time, and a comparison of the attorney to others in the office in terms of profitability. In some firms, the weekly billings and dollar value are distributed to all lawyers so that they can chart each other's progress. Notice how these programs focus exclusively on *quantitative* factors (time, money, profitability) to the exclusion of *qualitative* factors (service, client satisfaction). The unfortunate result of this hyperattention to timekeeping is that attorneys relate to time as if each instant were potentially billable. An attorney knows that each hour he spends on unbillable matters will detract from his yearly required billable hours. A one-hour lunch during working hours costs the attorney one hour off his daily requirement, and it costs the firm hundreds of dollars in potential billings. For most lawyers, time is quite literally money, and this means that lawyers see time as an asset that cannot be wasted. Attorneys police themselves by internalizing a punitive time clock in which all nonwork time is seen as wasteful.

From the fact that seven out of ten lawyers responding to a California survey would be willing to leave the profession tomorrow if given a feasible alternative,[42] we can surmise that most attorneys keep their jobs only as a way of holding onto a lifestyle to which they have become accustomed. In other words, they work in order to live, but do not find fulfillment in their legal practice. The bulk of their working day is devoted to activities disconnected from *themselves*.

The *third* type of alienation mentioned by Marx is estrangement from "species being," a term that designates man's special ability to work for reasons other than the satisfaction of physical means: "Man produces even when he is free from physical need and only truly produces in freedom therefrom."[43] The ability to transcend the task at hand, to redirect our instruments toward loftier goals, is what makes humans different from mere animals who repeat the same tasks endlessly without thinking of the ethical consequences. The sad truth is that lawyers have turned themselves into robots by shutting off all ethical and social considerations of their work. For most lawyers, the practice of law requires a brainwashed tunnel vision in favor of one's client and against the entire rest of the world.

Consider the tobacco litigation, by which large firms managed to delay some eight hundred separate lawsuits from coming to trial over a thirty-year period without a settlement or adverse ruling, by outspending, delaying, and burying the plaintiffs' lawyers in paperwork, all while sitting on top of internal documents establishing their clients' wrongdoing.[44] Or consider how Enron, the seventh-biggest corporation in America, employed an army of lawyers to evade taxes for a number of years through the meticulous exploitation of minuscule loopholes in the tax code. What else besides tunnel vision would enable a young lawyer to be part of a gigantic effort to set up nearly nine hundred subsidiary corporations in offshore locations, for the sole purpose of avoiding taxation? Tax-avoidance behavior that would be criminal if committed by a waitress at the neighborhood diner was somehow insulated as "legal" by a bevy of lawyers. Surely the lawyers who put this together are not dumb; they did it because they felt that they had no choice—either pursue the client's goals without criticism or quit the job and endure humiliation, anxiety, and bankruptcy. To speak out is too risky. In the Enron debacle, the lone in-house attorney who dared to ask questions was brutally excoriated by the chief executive officer.[45]

Faced with the choice of compliance or banishment, young lawyers find themselves taking extreme and outrageous positions for their clients under the broad excuse that the adversary system gives them permission to take any position that is not a blatant violation of the ethical rules. So young lawyers become adept at burying, concealing, veiling, delaying, obscuring, and insulating their clients. Let's face it—there is something wrong with a profession that reduces young lawyers to mere technocrats who cannot justify the consequences of their behavior other than to throw up their hands and point to some vague concept of an "adversary system" that presumably allows their well-funded clients to pummel every opponent into the ground.

The *fourth* type of alienation discussed by Marx is alienation from others.[46] Marx pointed out that each worker sees his fellows as competitors or consumers: "[E]very person speculates on creating a new need in another so as to drive him to a fresh sacrifice, to place him in a new dependence and to seduce him into a new mode of gratification and therefore economic ruin."[47] Each person is alienated to the point of not being able to see any alternative mode of life apart from being either a worker or owner. Like a slave who would rather become a slaveowner than abolish the institution of slavery, the worker cannot conceive any alternative to the existing situation:

> It is . . . quite natural . . . that the actual agents of production feel completely at home in these estranged and irrational forms . . . for these are precisely the configurations of appearance in which they move, and with which they are daily involved.[48]

> The advance of capitalist production develops a working class which by education, training and habit looks upon the requirements of that mode of production [wage-labor, private property, competition] as self-evident natural laws.[49]

Instead of recognizing that the entire system is flawed for producing so few property owners and so many propertyless workers, the worker does not blame the system itself, but holds out hope that one day she too can be an owner, an exploiter.

This type of alienation is played out in the willingness of firms to lay off associates when times are hard, something that was anathema in the old days. According to the authors of a sociological study on law firms from 1960 to 1990, "termination tended to be long-drawn-out and disguised," while outright firing was restricted to rare cases of specific wrongdoing.[50] Nowadays, termination can be immediate and needs no justification.

In the final analysis, alienation from others takes the form of not caring about *helping* clients as much as *possessing* clients. The primary desire among lawyers is to possess a portable client base, because this is the equivalent of the possession of capital. Further, lawyers prefer the business aspects of the profession to the nuts and bolts of actual legal work. This is evidenced by the fact that when attorneys rise to the status of "rainmaker" they invariably stop practicing law and focus on rainmaking. If given an opportunity, they will run from the practice of law. This means that lawyers do not really desire to work with other lawyers to solve problems for clients as much as they want to be in a position in which they command other lawyers. In other words, lawyers have become businessmen who are saddled with the unfortunate baggage of having to earn money by providing an actual service, which can be a nuisance if your main concern is money.

Suggestions for Change

We have seen that law has become more alienating as it has been transformed from a pre-capitalist guild into a full-blown capitalist wage-labor system. Lawyers now see themselves as workers instead of professionals, as creators of personal wealth instead of social good. Lawyers are scared by the recent changes in the legal profession, and they are "running from the law."[51]

Certainly, the American Bar Association must bear some of the blame for allowing the number of attorneys to expand beyond reason. It must decrease the number of law school graduates by curtailing the number of accredited law schools and demanding a reduction in enrollments. The number of law school graduates must be brought down so that it reflects the market demand for legal services. We live in an era where a startling number of young lawyers are unemployed, and we live in a country where there are too many lawyers by any standard. Under these conditions, there is no excuse for churning out forty thousand new attorneys every year.

Second, the ABA should either outlaw or strongly discourage the practice of billing by the hour for legal services. It is abundantly clear that this practice has enslaved attorneys to the demands of the clock and has turned them into high-tech wage slaves who must keep track of every telephone call and every quarter hour spent on a case. In addition, it turns each lawyer into a minicapitalist who constantly monitors his own profitability, like a hypochondriac who checks his pulse ten times a day. The billable-hour method is not a humane way to practice law, and it contributes to the commodification of the lawyer and the alienation of productive power.

Third, the national and local bar associations should underwrite loans to young lawyers so that they can open solo practices. At present, it is cost-prohibitive for a lawyer to strike out on her own. By guaranteeing loans to young lawyers, the bar associations will break down the class division which now exists between lawyers. Alternatively, law schools can underwrite loan repayments for students who agree to take jobs in the public sector or to set up neighborhood clinics. There has to be some economic mechanism to give young lawyers an incentive to serve the public. Let's face it: young lawyers in Chicago, New York City, and San Francisco cannot afford to work for Legal Aid at a salary averaging under $40,000, nor can they survive in a position with the district attorney's or public defender's office that typically pays under $50,000.[52] It is ridiculous to decry young lawyers' loss of public spirit and commitment to justice when there is no way for the lawyer to survive in the public interest sector or to open a neighborhood law office.

Fourth, lawyers should be mentored on the old apprenticeship model so that a young lawyer is paired with a partner and evaluated *together simultaneously* (as opposed to having the lawyer-mentor stand with the partners in passing judgment on the associate). The system needs to be constructed so that the failure of an associate is at the same time a failure of a partner as well. A mentoring program could also be started between established lawyers and law students.[53]

Finally, young attorneys should be given entire projects to work on, as opposed to small, random pieces of work, especially boring due diligence assignments and document production. They must be taught that their work is valuable and has a social function that affects real people beyond the immediate client.

In exchange for these reforms, young lawyers will have to accept cuts in starting salaries, and will have to stop evaluating law firms on the basis of how much they pay.

Lawyers have a monopoly on the ability to represent clients on legal matters, which means that they alone must bear responsibility for ensuring that all Americans have meaningful access to the courts. This requires substantial commitment on the part of law firms to handling low-profile, unglamorous pro bono work in the trenches; it means bringing poor people into the law firms and giving them the best possible service for free. Otherwise, lawyers (and law firms) are responsible for creating and perpetuating an unjust system that cannot live up to its own promise of equal justice. Let us not forget that there was once a time when the legal profession was esteemed precisely because it was something more than a mere economic enterprise.

And if the transformation of law into a business is a fait accompli, then we should open the profession to the free market by allowing paralegals and laypersons to represent clients. If the former president of the Colorado bar was correct that the profession is "on its way into a black hole of commercialism from which there is no return,"[54] then we might as well go all the way by allowing any college graduate with a paralegal degree to represent clients as long as they carry malpractice insurance. This would at least give rise to the emergence of quasi-lawyer professionals in sufficient numbers to guarantee affordable representation for all Americans.[55] Such a scheme would acknowledge openly what lawyers are afraid to admit: that the profession has become a business that benefits a small group of older lawyers (predominantly male, white, and propertied) at the expense of younger lawyers and to the detriment of ordinary citizens, who can no longer afford lawyers.

These comments suggest that the mere *environmental* or *structural* arrangements that predominate in the legal profession are to blame for making life miserable for young associates. That is, the status quo of legal practice in America produces unhappiness. In making this claim, I have purposely restricted my comments to *structural* factors and avoided talking about the horribly unpleasant *substantive* tasks that await young lawyers who work at firms, especially large firms. I deal with that subject in the next chapter.

chapter five:
The *Content* of Law Firm Practice: Doing Things You Don't Want to Do

The large law firm—with hundreds of attorneys in offices throughout the country—has emerged as the gold standard for the legal profession. Industry magazines such as *American Lawyer*, the *National Law Journal*, and the *American Bar Association Journal* carry endless stories about the fortunes of large law firms, especially the powerful firms based in New York City and Washington, D.C. Even the former dean of Yale Law School acknowledged that giant law firms "exercise an influence, both within the profession and outside it, that far exceeds [their] numerical strength."[1] For one thing, these firms are immensely profitable, often generating profits in excess of $1 million per partner per year, earned primarily from representing the nation's largest corporations, banks, and brokerage houses. Furthermore, law students hold these firms in high esteem because they recruit primarily from the top tier of law schools and pay the highest starting salaries. Even the general public is mesmerized, responding to surveys by indicating their belief that large firms are more competent and more ethical than smaller firms and solo practitioners.[2]

Given the positive attention lavished on large firms and their powerful clients, there is a growing need to explore the dark side of large-firm practice. Despite the opulent appearance and stately demeanor, big-firm practice is built upon misery and injustice. Young lawyers at large firms find themselves subservient to large corporate institutional clients, whom they try to impress by engaging in morally reprehensible tactics and naked abuses of power that they vainly rationalize with appeals to the "adversary system" and the "free market." Large law firms are structurally oriented to thwart any advancements for workers, consumers, and ordinary people. *They are injustice machines.*

The "big-firming" of the legal profession is a new development. Abe Lincoln practiced law with a single partner, whom Lincoln would annoy every day by arriving late and reading the newspaper out loud. By the start of the twentieth century, only a handful of firms had more than five partners. Even in the late 1950s, only twenty New York firms had more than fifty lawyers. And then things changed. By the early 1990s, there were well over a hundred New York firms with more than one hundred lawyers, and by 1995 the *average* number of attorneys at law firms in downtown Chicago was more than one hundred.[3] And in the last ten years, many of the largest law firms in America doubled in size, then doubled again, either by hiring more lawyers fresh out of school, by lateral hiring, or by mergers with other firms. Suddenly it was commonplace to hear about law firms with upwards of a thousand lawyers in offices worldwide.[4] These megafirms attract an inordinate amount of attention. When lawyers get together they generally gossip about what is going on at the large firms, and this is especially true for the younger lawyers, who are intensely aware of minuscule and frankly meaningless differences between the various large firms, often capable of reciting the starting salary and minimum number of billable hours required at each firm.

If you have any doubts about this, you should spend some time reading what young lawyers have to say on websites such as Greedy Associates or Vault, which are basically electronic sewing circles for young associates at big firms.

There is something a little odd when five hundred licensed professionals who have no connection to each other suddenly decide to become colleagues. As one partner described his immense firm, "It's a law firm of the 80s and 90s. You have a bunch of people tied together by money, and that's it."[5] No wonder these firms are perceived as "sweatshops" that work the associates to death in order to generate profits for the partners. This is the message in John Grisham's bestseller, *The Firm*, where the protagonist is told that he should bill heavily whenever he merely thinks about a client: even if the client crosses your mind in the shower, you can bill it as a strategy session.[6] The focus on moneymaking at large law firms has led some people to wonder how such outright greed can be reconciled with the ethical demands of the profession: "The subculture of the law firm does not put much emphasis on truth as a value. In large firms, earning money is valued above all else. Lawyers give up their private lives, consoling themselves with lavish salaries, perks, and fringe benefits. The structure of the work in large law firms places large firms on a collision course with many humanistic values such as truthfulness and altruism."[7] There is a direct correlation between the ascendency of large law firms and the growing impression that the legal profession is in a state of crisis. This is no coincidence; the two events are intimately connected. Put simply, large law firms systematically thwart justice by placing young lawyers in a pressure cooker of unrealistic expectations, causing the young lawyers to behave ruthlessly (and even unethically) to gain every advantage in the path toward partnership. Even the most scrupulous young lawyer is powerless before the demands of the voracious megafirm.

Large law firms serve the interests of powerful institutions who have time and money on their side: they stand to benefit by delaying meritorious claims and outspending any opponents into submission. The real losers in the equation are those poor individuals who have a legitimate claim against a large institution protected by a big law firm. There is nothing more depressing and disheartening than being a sole practitioner representing an ordinary person who happens to have a valid claim against, say, Circuit City or Wal-Mart. By the time your client gets her day in court, you will both be penniless and emotionally destroyed. As one lawyer for tobacco giant R. J. Reynolds admitted, "The way we won these cases was not by spending all of Reynolds' money, but by making the other son of a bitch spend all of his."[8] These tactics are applauded by big-firm lawyers who openly advocate a "winning is everything" attitude.[9]

The growth in the size of law firms is due to the advantages of economies of scale. It became clear in the 1980s that a *medium*-sized firm simply could not handle all of the, say, corporate or litigation work for a large client like Citibank or Prudential. Only by growing larger could a law firm simultaneously staff a number of gigantic deals for a range of powerful institutional clients. The strategy worked—the bigger firms attracted more clients—and so the formula was repeated endlessly in every major city until virtually all of the high-level legal work shifted from smaller firms to larger firms. The end result of this phenomenon is that gigantic corporations and financial institutions have placed most of their legal work in the hands of gigantic megafirms. In the process, lawyers at big firms have become immensely wealthy from serving the interests of institutional clients.

The trend toward bigger law firms creates horrific disparities in legal firepower. The giant megafirms and their clients have more resources than small-fry lawyers, and this power differential undermines the adversary system of justice, which is based on a model of equal firepower on both sides of a case. When one side has legions of lawyers, assistants, advisors, and investigators, and can wait indefinitely for the case to be tried, the scales of justice begin to tip impermissibly toward large companies and their law firms, who can out-spend, outmaneuver, outlast, out-lawyer and over-lawyer anyone who dares to challenge their clients. By contrast, lawyers who practice alone or in small firms tend to represent actual human people (that is, individuals) with limited resources. This is not a fair fight: big firms crush litigants who have less money. For example, many of the cases against the large tobacco companies were delayed for *decades* by the big firms. And when two giant firms are pitted against each other, the result is a never-ending, go-nowhere, paper war.

At their worst, large law firms are tunnel-vision profit machines that specialize in overkill, overbilling, delay, outspending, obfuscation, and generally standing in the way of justice. But since they are hugely profitable and allied with powerful interests, they enjoy an undeserved patina of legitimacy and social standing. This last point is paradoxical: large firms have allied themselves with the most corrupt elements in the business world, yet they are perceived as more ethical than solo attorneys.[10] This is due largely to packaging and marketing. We are prepared to laugh at the neighborhood lawyer with cheap plastic furniture who operates out of a storefront office on the West Side of Chicago, but we hesitate to question the legitimacy of a giant firm with impeccable office space and tasteful decor, even if the firm made its money representing corporate crooks at Enron, WorldCom, and other corporations that have been exposed for massive fraud. The giant law firm with offices atop the skyscraper has the money and the social standing to support its smug, comfortable, and bourgeois WASP identity, but behind the veil is a relentless cruelty in the service of business interests at the expense of individuals.

This point must be made clear: big firms are in the business of *enabling* their clients to twist the legal process against the interests of ordinary people. They do this through unethical litigation tactics and by setting up questionable business arrangements. By way of example, the Bloomberg business wire recently ran a story describing how the chief executive officer of Kmart

Corporation stands to receive a $9.5-million severance package for services rendered while the company fell into bankruptcy, at the same time that ordinary workers were laid off *en masse*.[11] Even though the word "lawyer" is nowhere mentioned, this transaction was undoubtedly orchestrated by lawyers at the expense of workers, consumers, creditors, and shareholders. On other occasions, lawyers own up to their skullduggery, as occurred recently when corporate lawyers openly acknowledged that they were redrafting their clients' severance agreements to provide that severance would be payable even if the executives commit a *felony* in the course of their job.[12] It is all legal, perhaps, yet it illustrates the pernicious, subtle, bloodless, behind-the-scene injustice that occurs when corporate lawyers favor the interests of management. Similarly, lawyers are the *enablers* for the wildly unjust salaries and perks of corporate managers. The average CEO of a major corporation now gets $10.8 million a year, an almost twentyfold increase since 1981, and more than four hundred times what an average worker makes.[13] This barbaric disparity puts to shame anything from the days of feudalism, and it is mediated through the law, specifically through the big law firms.

Or consider the case of a worker at a Circuit City in California who tried to sue the company for discrimination. Circuit City moved to dismiss the Complaint on the grounds that the employee was bound by an arbitration agreement tucked away into the corner of a standard form contract that all employees were forced to sign in order to keep their jobs.[14] Circuit City had drafted the arbitration clause and other one-sided provisions to prevent employees from suing in a real court to establish a public record and legal precedent against the company; and since most poor people are desperate for work, they will sign anything in order to earn a wage. Eventually, many years after bringing his claim for discrimination, the employee finally won the right to have his claim heard in a bona fide court of law—something that is guaranteed to every single American by the Constitution. How hard did Circuit City fight against its own employee in order to deny his rights? The case started in federal court in California, then went to federal appellate court in California, then went to the United States Supreme Court, and then went back to the federal appellate court in California. After an incredibly expensive court battle lasting years, fought tooth and nail by Circuit City, the plaintiff was finally restored to basic civil rights and allowed to sue in a real court instead of having to pay in advance for a vague arbitration hearing. The message to employees and consumers is clear: the deck is stacked against you to begin with, and if you try to upset the apple cart by challenging the company, it will take years off your life.

These are merely two small examples of everyday injustices that are perpetrated by large law firms on behalf of institutional clients. Imagine this type of work repeated by thousands of giant firms across the country, literally around the clock, and you get some idea of how the legal system becomes tilted in favor of institutions.

From a standpoint of pure quality, large law firms are capable of excellent legal work, for two reasons. First, most of the lawyers at top firms graduated from leading law schools, so they are highly intelligent to begin with. Second, their clients have a tremendous amount of money to spend for legal work, so the lawyers can afford to subspecialize and take time to explore every nuance of every matter, obtaining a level of expertise rarely matched by small firms and solo practitioners. But just as size magnifies the *achievements* of a large firm, it also exaggerates their worst *excesses*, including the use of dirty tricks on a massive scale. I am speaking not only of blatant wrongdoing such as massive overbilling and conversion of client funds (which are endemic at large firms), but more subtly with regard to the game playing that characterizes the antics of large firms. This chapter explains how law firms systematically thwart justice by outspending their opponents, stonewalling justified claims, setting up byzantine Ponzi schemes, and drafting business contracts that unfairly crush weaker parties. But first, we need to understand the group dynamics that make young lawyers at firms so willing to do this type of work. In other words, how does a young lawyer with the best of intentions suddenly find herself doing things that she knows on some level to be morally wrong?

Group Dynamics and Mass Hysteria

Like all gigantic single-minded institutions (the army and the police department come to mind), law firms take advantage of the hidden fascism within each of us. They provide an all-purpose, ready-made protocol to young lawyers who pass through their doors. Just as the gates of Dante's Inferno proclaimed "Abandon Hope All Ye Who Enter," the large law firms send the message that young associates should set aside all moral, social, and economic qualms about their work and simply find the best technical solution to the client's wishes. Young lawyers are exempted from asking questions such as, "Is this merger going to be fair to the employees of the target company?," "Is this litigation tactic fair to the other side?," "Is it morally acceptable for us to shelter all of the corporation's income?," "Is this employee handbook fair?," "Is this executive stock option plan wasteful?," or "Does the business have a duty to keep the factory in this community instead of opening a sweatshop in Haiti?" These complex, nuanced questions are replaced with a single mantra—"If the client wants it and is willing to pay for it, and it isn't a clear violation of the law, then we'll do it." If the client wants to avoid taxation by setting up nine hundred subsidiary corporations in the Caribbean (as was the case with Enron), then so be it, let's set them up.[15] If Circuit City wants to force all of its employees into mandatory arbitration based on boilerplate language that no one can understand, then so be it, we'll draft the language.[16] It comes down to the soldier's creed: 'Ours not to question why, ours but to do or die.' In fact, when I was a second-year associate, I was told by a senior associate, "When the managing partner tells me to jump, I don't ask why, I just say 'How high, Sir?'"

The soldier's creed may be fine in the army, where too much moral reflection can cause a soldier to hesitate and endanger an entire squadron of men. But lawyers are not soldiers. The Rules of Professional Responsibility specifically permit lawyers to raise ethical and moral issues about their clients' behavior and to persuade the clients to modify their original objectives.[17] Lawyers rarely exercise this power for fear of alienating the client, on the belief that no client wants to be second-guessed by a lawyer. Instead, lawyers tend to hide behind the language in the Rules which allows them to behave like hired guns so long as they don't actually counsel the client to do something fraudulent or illegal. Here is the key language that absolves lawyers of moral responsibility:

> Rule 1.2. (a) A lawyer shall abide by a client's decisions concerning the objectives of representation, and shall consult with the client on the means by which they are to be pursued. . . . (b) A lawyer's representation of a client does not constitute an endorsement of the client's political, economic, social or moral views or activities. . . . (d) A lawyer shall not counsel a client to engage, or assist a client, in conduct the lawyer knows is criminal or fraudulent.

This lays the groundwork for avoiding all the hard questions about what a client wants to do. First, the lawyer can claim that the client has already set the "ends" of representation and the lawyer merely handles the "means." Second, the lawyer can claim that it is the client (and not the lawyer) who is responsible for the moral, social, and political consequences. Finally, any individual attorney can absolve herself from guilt by claiming that she is merely doing the bidding of the firm, so it is not really she who is enabling the client's actions. Simultaneously, the client is telling itself that its actions are fully justified because the lawyers haven't raised any objections—so the client and the lawyers are caught in a *folie à deux*. In the end, the attorney comes to resemble Henri Sanson, the Executioner of Paris, who was appointed by Louis XVI on behalf of the *ancien régime*, then switched sides after the French Revolution, beheading his former employers.[18] When Sanson was accused of hypocrisy and moral indifference, he simply replied that he was a mere instrument put into motion by others. This is how lawyers distance themselves from the pernicious actions of their clients—they claim to be mere technocrats who cannot be held accountable for the damage caused by their clients. And they also hide behind their clients and their firm, absolving themselves of individual responsibility. This is undoubtedly how the lawyers at Vinson & Elkins and Kirkland & Ellis justified their behavior when setting up lavish perks and Ponzi schemes for Enron and its subsidiaries. Their legal work ruined the lives of hundreds, perhaps thousands, of workers, yet they have never accepted any responsibility for wrongdoing. A similar myopia occurred in the Tyco International scandal, in which two executives were paid half a billion dollars under suspicious circumstances, and their lawyer argued that there could not be anything fraudulent going on since the transactions were fully disclosed and approved by the board of directors, the accountants, and the lawyers.[19] In other words, the injustice has become legalized, which is precisely the hallmark of corrupt regimes. How is it possible for a lawyer to take pride in setting up a corporate structure where the happiness of a few insiders is built upon the immiseration and impoverishment of countless outsiders? How is it possible that these lawyers are considered supremely ethical and worthy of respect while the profession and the general public frown upon defense lawyers who represent drug dealers— lawyers who at least are in the business of making sure that their clients have basic constitutional rights?

Whenever people are put in a group setting (such as a law firm), they start to lose all sense of individual responsibility. A classic example of this is the Holocaust, where Germans as a group behaved in a way that few Germans would have behaved on their own. The principle is well-documented: the larger the group, the less restrained by individual conscience, ethics, or guilt. In effect, the individual is seduced by the power of the group into a feeling of invincibility. This was first noted by sociologist Gustav Le Bon in his groundbreaking work on crowds: "The individual forming part of a group acquires, solely from numerical considerations, a sentiment of invincible power, which allows him to yield to instincts which, had he been alone, he would perforce have kept under restraint. He will be the less disposed to check himself, from the consideration that, a group being anonymous and in consequence irresponsible, the sentiment of responsibility which always controls individuals disappears entirely."[20] Lawyers in big firms feel so empowered by the size of their firm and the power of their clients that they find themselves involved in unethical practices that they would never have undertaken if they were working in a small firm. The big-firming of the profession makes the profession less ethical.

A superb illustration of how the individual hides behind a group is the trial of Adolph Eichmann, the architect for the mass internment and execution of Jews throughout Europe. When he was finally hauled before the International Court at Nuremberg, Eichmann proclaimed that he was not anti-Semitic but merely doing his job as a bureaucrat: "Once again I would stress that I am guilty of being obedient, having subordinated myself to my official duties and the obligations of service under my oath of allegiance and my oath of office. . . . I did not persecute Jews with avidity and passion. That is what the government did."[21] In other words, "I am not responsible for what my client (the government) asks me to do." Reporting on the trial, philosopher Hannah Arendt proclaimed that Eichmann illustrated the "banality of evil," the capacity of ordinary bureaucrats to participate in mass injustices.[22] This was the excuse of choice for collaborators who justified their behavior as merely doing their job or performing a service, absolving themselves from responsibility by insisting on their merely instrumental role. Even though such people were in the service of the government, and therefore agents of the government, they reasoned that it was the government itself (and not they as individuals) who was responsible. This was seen in the behavior of the automobile mechanics and designers of the vans in which Jews were gassed to death:

> Specialists whose expertise normally had nothing to do with mass murder suddenly found themselves a minor cog in the machinery of destruction. Occupied with procuring, dispatching, maintaining, and repairing motor vehicles, their expertise and facilities were suddenly pressed into the service of mass murder when they were charged with procuring gas vans. . . . What disturbed them most was the criticism and complaints [from Nazis] about faults in their product. The shortcomings of the gas vans were a negative reflection on their workmanship that had to be remedied. Kept fully abreast of the problems arising in the field, they strove for ingenious technical adjustments to make their product more efficient and acceptable to its operators.[23]

Sociologist Robert Merton referred to this phenomenon as *displacement of goals*: "Adherence to rules, originally conceived as a means, becomes transformed into an end-in-itself."[24]

It is important to understand that all of us (not just Nazis and Klan members) have this element to our personality. This was clearly demonstrated in the Milgram experiments at Yale University in the early 1960s, where professor Stanley Milgram brought in people off the street to participate in experiments in which they were asked to administer electric shocks to innocent victims (the shocks were fake; the victims were actors).[25] Milgram found that an amazing percentage of ordinary Americans from all walks of life administered the shocks with increasing voltages, on the grounds that they were simply performing an assigned role, or helping out with a research project, or earning their pay for participating in the project. Interestingly, Milgram found that people were loath to administer the shocks if the experiment was altered slightly to require holding the subject's hand onto the "electric" device. In other words, people find it much easier to administer shocks from behind a glass window (at a distance, that is), and when they have some vague overriding justification to rationalize their conduct.

This is precisely how law firms get young lawyers to do terrible things. Nobody commands lawyers to lose their ethical restraints or their moral conscience—they do it on their own to keep their jobs. There is simply no other way to explain why so many young lawyers spend their days thwarting justice by doing the bidding of large corporate interests. And it is always done from a distance, indirectly, and with the utmost decorum: a lawyer sits in a plush office and dreams up legal strategies for a corporate client that have the effect of crippling workers, consumers, and the community. These lawyers tell themselves that everything they do is "legal"—but this is a lame excuse. Slavery was once "legal," and so were sexual harassment, the internment of Japanese during World War II, forced sterilizations, and spousal rape. It is a cop-out to insulate one's behavior under the rubric of legality.

Lawyers generally distance themselves from their actions by adopting rationalizations. First, they claim that the adversary system demands that they represent their clients zealously, and second, a lawyer is permitted to take any position or use any tactic so long as he doesn't violate the Rules of Professional Responsibility. This is otherwise known as the "adversary system excuse"[26] and it becomes a blunt instrument in the hands of lawyers who mistakenly think that it authorizes all manner of twisting, delay, shading, harassing, and manipulating. Virtually every lawyer who does something unethical (shredding documents, coaching witnesses, invading privacy, filing frivolous claims) will wrap himself in the flag of the adversary system. In reality, however, there is not a shred of support for the idea that the adversary system leads to justice or truth. In a society where individuals are pitted against giant corporations, the party with the most money and legal firepower ends up getting more "justice" and "truth." Appealing to an adversary system that is broken does not solve anything.

The Rules of Professional Responsibility do not set meaningful limits on lawyers' misconduct. The rules are extremely permissive and hopelessly vague. Short of outright lying and destroying evidence, lawyers are free to get away with almost anything. As if to let lawyers off the hook, the rules are written in a wishy-washy format that does not solve dilemmas so much as restate them in vanilla terms; for example, a lawyer is admonished to be "fair" to opposing counsel and make "reasonable efforts to expedite litigation." She must assert claims only if there is a "good faith argument" to support them, and she must charge a "reasonable fee." You get the idea: the rules say nothing about the everyday tactics of delay, obfuscation, and discovery abuse that make up the bread and butter of big-firm practice. Even worse, the rules are virtually silent on the practice of corporate law, so there is nothing to prevent lawyers from drafting one-sided and self-serving contracts. And the state bar authorities almost never clamp down on a lawyer for ordinary, garden-variety obfuscation, harassment, and delay, because the ethical rules are written so vaguely that any half-decent lawyer could argue that his actions were justified under the circumstances.

Judges have the power to enforce the Rules of Professional Responsibility *sua sponte* and to punish lawyers for misbehavior, but they rarely do so. Much has been written about Rule 11 of the Federal Rules of Civil Procedure (and state law equivalents), which were designed to facilitate sanctions against lawyers who put forth unmeritorious claims. Don't hold your breath. Indeed, the Supreme Court of the United States has recognized that the adversary system sometimes compels lawyers to create confusion in favor of their clients: "Under our adversary system the role of counsel is not to make sure the truth is ascertained but to advance his client's cause by ethical means. . . . Within the limits of professional propriety, causing delay and sowing confusion not only are his right but may be his duty."[27] That is from the United States Supreme Court. Here is what a well-known federal appellate judge had to say on the likelihood of punishing a lawyer for filing a frivolous claim: "[S]omething is frivolous only when (a) we've decided the very point, and recently, against the person reasserting it, or (b) ninety-nine out of one hundred practicing lawyers would be ninety-nine percent sure that the position is untenable, and the other one percent would be sixty percent sure it's untenable."[28] These two quotations, without more, are enough to rationalize almost any action by an attorney. The odds of being sanctioned are so low that it is almost malpractice not to bend the ethical rules. In the end, lawyers become mere instruments, stripped of critical thinking, blindly pursuing their client's interest, and disowning moral responsibility for their own actions.

But no one is really fooled by this exercise in role playing. Lawsuits do not handle themselves, and contracts do not write themselves: it takes a lawyer to do these things. And in the end, a lawyer is responsible for what she *enables*: that is the whole reason that we have a concept of "conspiracy" in criminal law, and "vicarious liability" in tort law. As for my own experience at a big firm, I felt crushed by the weight of responsibility for the injustices that I was enabling through my legal services. Let me tell you precisely how it feels to work at a large firm.

Litigation: Outspending Your Opponents Until They Collapse

During law school, I clerked at a large firm in Chicago, a firm that I would later join as an attorney. The lawyers at this firm were top-notch, so my skills were finely honed over the years. In addition, I received a crash course in big-firm socialization. My first object lesson was that I should remain forever distant from and unconcerned with the actual facts of a case, and that I should filter everything through the gloss provided by the partners and the clients.

On my first day as a summer associate, I was called into the office of a senior partner to receive an assignment. The case was staffed with one partner, two senior associates, and a junior associate. I was exceptionally nervous and excited at the same time; I could not believe that I was about to get a real case, that my actions were going to affect the lives of actual people. After spending my first year of law school writing legal memoranda for clients with fake names, I would finally get a case in the real world.

It is difficult to convey the petty fears and uncertainties that pass through the minds of summer associates. They worry about the most mundane things like which chair to sit in when entering a partner's office, whether to call junior associates by their first name, how much cologne to wear, how loudly one should laugh, whether to swear when the time is right, even how to stand and walk like a lawyer. All of this process of adaptation is going on apart from the more serious worries about how long one should take on a project, how forcefully one should phrase one's findings, and so on. There is a challenge of learning a new language and research skills, but also of picking up a set of social skills and subtle clues about how lawyers behave.

Once I had been introduced to the lawyers with whom I would be working, the senior partner told me that our client was a major Chicago hospital and that I would be given a research project in a lawsuit accusing the hospital of "constructive discharge." I immediately panicked because I had never heard of constructive discharge. I confessed my ignorance, and the partner explained that constructive discharge is transferring employees to undesirable jobs in an effort to get them to quit. Our client was being sued by a nurse who alleged that she had been constructively discharged. Specifically, she alleged that after working at the hospital for seven years, she got pregnant and found herself transferred to a much lower-paying position that required odd hours. Eventually this woman was given such bizarre hours that she quit. But since she was not fired, as such, she could not sue for wrongful termination, and that is why she had brought the claim for constructive discharge. She felt that the hospital had a policy of mistreating pregnant workers. Our client, the hospital, wanted to defend the case on the grounds that the move was economically motived as part of a restructuring of the staff and had nothing to do with prejudice against her for being pregnant. The hospital, I was told, did not want to set a precedent for caving in to lawsuits by employees. They wanted to have the case dismissed or settled for nuisance value. My assignment was to see if we could find some way to force a dismissal or settlement.

I was handed a thick file that contained all of the correspondence and pleadings in the case, plus all of the notes and prior memoranda of law. I was told to research the constructive discharge claim and come up with material for a strong letter that we would give to the opposing lawyer in a meeting that was scheduled in three weeks.

I took the file back to my cubicle and opened it up. I was immediately struck by how rich the facts were in comparison to the facts in the assignments that I had received in law school, which were basically given to me in a canned format. Here were so many different pieces of the puzzle: letters between the employee and her supervisors setting forth conflicting versions of events, statements from the hospital administration about the need for restructuring the staff, interoffice memos from the hospital, medical records, employee time sheets, and so on. It struck me that for the first time I was actually seeing an entire dispute unfold before my eyes, something that I had not seen in law school. Indeed, in law school I read only appellate case decisions, and in legal writing class I did not see a full case file. Seeing all of this information in one place was exciting. I was seeing a real-life conflict. I sat back and thought about the woman who had brought the suit, where she lived and what she was thinking right now, and also about the directors of the hospital, how they were relying on us to come through for them.

I spent the next week researching at a fever pitch: I even worked at night at the law school, consulting treatises and decisions from other jurisdictions. By the end of the week I had prepared a clear memo. I argued that the Complaint failed to allege all of the elements of a constructive discharge claim, that the case law supported the hospital's defense that the plaintiff was reassigned in a bona fide restructuring, and that the plaintiff would face a severe burden of proof at trial in making the claim for constructive discharge.

I submitted the memorandum and went on to other research projects, but was called back to the partner's office in one week to review the memorandum. The two of us sat down and he walked me through the memorandum for a full hour. The entire memo had been covered in blue ink to show his corrections. We went over it step by step, and at every stage he showed me how the memo could have been improved: how I had failed to fully cite a case, how I had used the passive voice too often, how in one instance I had cited dicta instead of a holding. I walked away somewhat embarrassed, feeling that I had wasted this man's time on my shoddy work. The memo was the best thing that I could produce, and it was still full of holes! He told me to revise the memorandum and use it to create a long letter to the opposing lawyer, threatening aggressive defense of litigation and suggesting that they should settle the case. I apologized profusely for my mistakes, and he comforted me by saying that I had done a nice job and that I would learn some of the tricks of the trade over the summer.

Several weeks after completing the letter, I was called back to the partner's office for a meeting. At the meeting I was informed that my memo and letter had proven very useful. The partner had convinced the opposing lawyer that if the case was going to proceed he would need to revise the Complaint or we would move to strike it as deficient, and that the plaintiff would probably lose at trial. Accordingly, a settlement was reached at a very low figure. The client was happy. The partner was happy. It was a great day in Western Civilization.

As I walked away from that meeting I felt like I was walking on clouds. Here I was wearing a suit in downtown Chicago, and full-blown lawyers were taking my work seriously! And in just one month's time, I could sense that my work was improving, that I was getting better at this game every day. I felt confident that with enough hard work and coaching, I could become a good lawyer, a person of power and respect.

That feeling lasted for only about an hour, however. By the time I reached my cubicle, the exultation had given way to perplexity and confusion. True, I had seen the case file and reviewed the correspondence, and I had done some genuine legal work in the real world, but how much did I really know about the case?

I had been assuming that the plaintiff had been trying to swindle the hospital with a bogus claim, that the lawsuit was filed as a nuisance and should have been settled for nuisance value. But what basis did I have for this conclusion? It struck me that I had bought the hospital's version of events hook, line, and sinker, perhaps because everyone at the firm was so convinced that the hospital was in the right. But the hospital was paying our bills, so perhaps our own vision was distorted. Maybe the hospital was wrong.

Slowly I began to wonder whether my work had been part of a massive effort to frighten a woman who had just given birth and lost a job. After all, we sent an exhaustive, long-winded, and citation-heavy letter on firm stationery to some small-fry lawyer on the South Side. The power differential between our side and the plaintiff's side was so great that perhaps they settled not because of my great legal work but because she was afraid of the cost of going up against our firm. Perhaps she was scared of the fact that we were a massive firm with massive resources and an impressive letterhead boasting of offices throughout the country (indeed, the letterhead scared me when I first saw it). If this were true, then it was not the law itself that was controlling the situation, but economics. The hospital had the money and hence the law on its side; we could afford to stall indefinitely and haggle over the tiniest legal issues, whereas the plaintiff needed to resolve the case to get on with her life. Yet the case was settled for nuisance value, so in the end it went down in history as a nuisance lawsuit. I wondered how it felt for this woman to believe that a great injustice had been committed against her, only to be swept aside as a nuisance.

On one level, I was very proud of my work. I was also pleased with my salary and the respect that I had earned from the great lawyers at the firm. And make no mistake, I respected these lawyers. They used a different kind of reasoning than my law school professors—more cutting, more exact, tougher, quicker to distinguish cases, always thinking of ways to gain an advantage. I was impressed with their ability to play every single angle of a lawsuit, to spot every potential avenue for victory or settlement. I considered it a privilege to simply watch them think out loud and strategize a case. But I also had some nagging doubts about the system as a whole.

These doubts were brought to the fore in my first true litigation assignment. Within a day of joining the firm as an associate, I found myself seated at a giant conference table in downtown Chicago, with nearly a dozen high-priced lawyers making upwards of $250 per hour, in a giant strategy session to find some way to avoid paying a $250,000 insurance claim to a man who had been disabled in a motorcycle accident.

The case was very simple. Our client was a national insurance company. We were defending a claim by a man living in California who had motorcycle insurance. One day while riding his motorcycle, he was blindsided, and paralyzed from the waist down. He was unable to have sex. He and his wife were beneficiaries of an insurance policy that covered "lack of consortium," the inability to have sex. The wife asked for $250,000, the policy limit for lack of consortium. There was no question that the man was medically incapable of sex, that he had paid all premiums due on the policy, and that he was not at fault in the accident.

And yet the insurance company—our client—refused to pay. It turns out that the insurance company had sent this man a flyer accompanying one of its billing statements (the type of junk flyer that nobody reads), and in minuscule print the flyer proclaimed that the insurance company no longer covered a spouse's consortium claim. Based on this disclaimer, which no one could have noticed, the company denied coverage. And just like that, the paralyzed man (and his wife) were abandoned by the insurance company.

Undeterred, the paralyzed man filed suit against our client in California state court. We lost the case. The judge ruled that our client's disclaimer language in the flyer was inconspicuous and therefore did not become part of the insurance contract. We appealed. The appellate court affirmed the ruling in favor of the paralyzed man, for the same reason as the trial court. We appealed. The California Supreme Court ruled once again for the paralyzed man, for the same reason.

And that is how the case arrived at my doorstep. The client wanted to know what remedy was available to avoid paying this claim. They had no personal animosity toward the paralyzed policyholder or his wife, but they didn't want to let stand the legal precedent that small language in a flyer was "inconspicuous" and therefore not legally binding. If that precedent became law, then the insurance company, indeed *all* insurance companies, were in big trouble because they were in the habit of unilaterally changing their policies after the fact by sending flyers to customers. They were ready to take this case all the way to the United States Supreme Court (the only court left that could hear an appeal) if they could only find a way to invoke the jurisdiction of the Supreme Court; otherwise, they stood ready to petition the California Supreme Court to reconsider its ruling. That's where I came in. My job was to find some way to prolong the case, erase the precedents against our client, or somehow derail the case at this late stage. I was given a week to write a memorandum proposing a solution.

I worked hard on this case, but it was rough because every moral sentiment in my body was on the side of the victim. The insurance company—our client—was being cruel and petty. I couldn't accept that I was being paid an astronomic amount of money to work at cross-purposes to some disabled guy who had the courage to wrestle an insurance company through the California court system. I admired the guy; and now I had to find a way to make his life even worse. In the end, I slapped together a mediocre memo recommending that the insurance company seek a rehearing from the California Supreme Court, but this was a lackluster recommendation that I knew would fail. The bottom line is that after reviewing the facts and the legal precedents, and after reading the California decisions in favor of the paralyzed man, I had completely identified with the other side and could see no logic in the position we were taking. And I found it disgusting that the insurance company considered its own customer as an enemy.

A week later I got a call from the lead partner on the case. He wanted to talk about my memorandum. As he went over it line by line, I could see that he was becoming increasingly frustrated with my work and my lack of aggressiveness. He wanted me to feel outraged at the injustice done to our client. *We* were the victims here, he told me. Our client had clearly disclaimed the coverage for lack of consortium only to be second-guessed by the weak-willed California judiciary, all because a motorcycle driver was too lazy to read his mail. He felt that I had read the precedents too conservatively, and now it would be up to him to rewrite the memo in a stronger and more straightforward manner before it could be sent to the client. He said, "The client doesn't want to hear that we have nothing more to do—they want to hear that we will fight to the end, and that the law is on our side." I sat there squirming and began to sweat, and I remember the feeling of the sweat under my arms and the feeling of the collar ripping into my neck as I dealt with the realization that I'd done a shoddy job on the memorandum because I simply didn't agree with the position that we were taking.

By this time, I had put together a pretty good picture of how litigation was played at big firms. Almost all of our work was defensive—the protection of large corporations. Most of the plaintiffs who sued our clients were middle-class people who lacked the funds for a protracted legal battle. As I worked on case after case, it seemed that we often engaged in the most dubious sorts of delay tactics. For example, our first move in virtually every case was to review the Complaint for minuscule and utterly harmless defects so that we could move to dismiss. I always had this job since I was the lowest man on the totem pole. I would sit at my desk with a copy of the Complaint in my left hand and the Civil Practice Act in my right hand, and I would simply pore over every word in the Complaint looking for a sign of weakness that could be challenged. If I was lucky, I would find a problem such as the failure to allege all of the elements of a cause of action in separate paragraphs, failure to allege a condition precedent, or failure to allege venue. My customary tactic was to find mundane, innocent problems like the failure to attach a copy of a contract cited in the Complaint, failure to break each allegation into a separate paragraph, failure to clearly separate the various counts, and other purely procedural defects. Our goal was to force the plaintiff to revise the Complaint two or three times over a period of several years, at a huge cost and delay. We told the court that we couldn't understand the Complaint because it was drafted so poorly. But of course we understood the Complaint perfectly from day one, and the defects that we pointed out were totally harmless. We insisted on our legal right that the Complaint be letter perfect under the Civil Practice Act, even if that meant stalling the case forever.

Once the Complaint had been revised, we moved immediately for judgment on the pleadings, alleging that the case should be dismissed on the basis of the pleadings considered in isolation from the underlying facts of the case. We knew that this motion is rarely granted, but so what? We had nothing to lose in asking for it anyway, if the client was willing to pay. We then launched into discovery mode, burying the other side with a blizzard of interrogatories and production requests, with enough detail to keep a team of people busy for months just to answer our questions and produce the documents that we requested. Our specialty was to ask for information that was borderline relevant but arduous and embarrassing to produce. For example, if the plaintiff claimed emotional trauma (as is very common), we would ask the plaintiff to produce extremely personal information including the name, address, phone number, diagnosis, summary, and so on, of every physician, counselor, or therapist the plaintiff had ever seen; every drug ever taken; the names, addresses, and contact information of every supervisor for every job they ever held; the contact information for ex-spouses, and so forth, until the plaintiff's entire private life had been laid bare. If this was not enough, we would depose the plaintiff for several days, grilling him with brutal questions about his private life that we dug up from investigators. In these depositions, I saw plaintiffs completely paralyzed and sweating after thirty minutes, often dismissing or settling the case then and there.

If all of that did not work, we would move for summary judgment by hitting the other side with an extremely long and detailed motion that cited dozens of cases and could only be answered at great cost. It didn't really matter whether the motion was credible, or whether we had a 5 percent or 70 percent chance of winning it—the goal was simply to destroy the other side by burying it in detail and busywork. At a minimum, the other side would have to look up each of the cases and distinguish them, a task costing thousands of dollars. Mind you, these motions were not slapped together haphazardly—they were expertly organized and beautifully argued. And we would send courtesy copies of these beautiful documents to the judge and his law clerks, knowing that the other side could not afford to do the same. If the motion failed, then we would prepare for trial by putting together a pretrial memorandum and by assembling a massive number of exhibits and expert witnesses. All in all, it was the equivalent of preparing for a high-tech war. It came as no surprise that we "won" every case: our clients had unlimited funds, and we could appeal every adverse ruling.

I had seen enough of litigation. I put in for a full-time transfer to the corporate department. In that department I discovered that corporate lawyers were not directly involved on the front lines of facing down injured plaintiffs, but instead were busy setting up a legal framework by which corporate executives always come out ahead of everybody else. I also found that the entire practice of corporate law rests on a sleight of hand. Even though our client was technically the corporation itself (as an entity), and even though our legal fees were paid by the corporation itself, virtually all of our time was spent catering to a select cadre of corporate officers and directors. Despite the fact that, say, Sears has fifty thousand employees, we did not represent all of them, only the top five executives. We would cater to these men shamelessly, then tell ourselves that we were representing the *company* as a whole. In a straight-up bald-faced lie, we would tell these executives that it would be a great benefit to the *company* if they were awarded golden parachutes and lavish stock options to continue providing their sage wisdom to the corporation, even though sales had plummeted on their watch. They must have known that it was a lie, but both sides were lying to each other, so there was nobody who was willing to call the other side to account.

Transactional Law: Setting the Framework for an Unjust System

My first transactional assignment was to provide support on the leveraged buyout of a trucking company. Our client was a large Chicago bank that was financing the corporate executives to buy all the company stock on the stock exchange, elect themselves to high offices and give themselves huge perks, then sell off the key assets and lay off employees to shake loose the cash needed to repay the loan.

Who stood to gain from this transaction? Let's see: a handful of executives, an investment banking firm, a bank, and two law firms.

Who stood to lose? Let's see: the employees who had devoted their life to the company and who would now be jobless, the clients of the company who would subsidize the deal by paying higher prices, and the community surrounding the trucking company. Not a single new product or service would be created. It was a purely paper transaction that had no economic justification. After this process of taking the company "private," the same people would turn around and take the company "public" again and make fresh millions. And once again, not a single new product or service would be created. All of the lawyers were clueless as to *why* we were doing the transaction—we only knew that they were paying us top dollar to get it done.

My immediate task was to travel to the corporate headquarters and conduct a "due diligence" review of the business, keeping an eye out for any legal problems that would be triggered by the proposed transaction. After putting together a due diligence report, I would help the senior associates draft the key documents in the deal.

So it was that I found myself in the basement of a corporate headquarters in suburban Detroit sifting through mounds of paperwork. The routine was numbing; the documents were boring. There were two highlights to my day: working out at the hotel gym in the morning, then drinking a big glass of brandy before bedtime. After assembling all the data, I went back to Chicago and wrote a long memorandum stating what I had found. This process took several weeks as I charted every subsidiary corporation and every relationship between the subsidiaries and the parent, along with every insurance policy and every asset owned by the corporation. This was one of the most mind-numbing experiences of my life, but it is one I would repeat over and over again. The end result of this labor was a very long memorandum which detailed all of the corporation's assets so that they could be properly encumbered during the leverage buyout. Once this was done, I began helping out the senior lawyers by drafting some of the legal documents for the transaction. After endless redrafting sessions and several all-nighters, the deal finally closed.

When the whole thing was done, I felt immense pride in the technical side of my work, and I was impressed by my own ability to work so hard. But something was missing—a *purpose*. I had literally no idea *why* the transaction was occurring in the first place. Here was a perfectly decent trucking company. Why did it need to go through a leveraged buyout? The party line was that the client needed to "take the company private" (that is, buy up all the stock) so that it would not be taken over by hostile speculators who would dismantle the company. But from where I stood, it seemed as if we were doing the exact same thing, only it was a *coup* from within rather than an attack from outside. As for the larger question of whether it was morally acceptable to design a transaction that destroyed jobs and hurt the community, no one dared to raise the issue.

Still, I found corporate law more rewarding than litigation, because I was building something for the future instead of quibbling over the past. It is less adversarial as well, and it is often more intellectual because it is more abstract and there are more parties involved. And since you are drafting the ground rules for relationships, there is a strong element of creativity. Over the years, I became proficient at drafting all manner of corporate documents, including asset purchase agreements, stock purchase agreements, resolutions, leases, employment agreements, partnership agreements, and so forth. Gradually I worked my way up to more complicated documents such as poison pills and securities offerings. Before I knew it, I was a bona fide associate in corporate law.

It slowly dawned on me that corporate lawyers live in a bubble—a black-

and-white universe where the clients are always right and everyone else is wrong. We would spend endless hours dreaming up new ways to enrich executives while the lowly workers were always employed at will and could be fired for any reason. We attended to the managers in fawning detail, always suggesting that the company adopt a new stock option plan, an incentive plan, a bonus plan, and so forth. In the name of protecting the *company*, we were looting the shareholders, discarding the workers, and constantly manipulating politicians to pass sympathetic legislation.

The key tool of the corporate lawyer is disguise: she learns to draft corporate documents (employee handbooks, employment agreements, press releases, annual reports, and the like) in such a way that nobody can see how unfair they are. We drafted everything so abstractly, so indirectly, so opaquely, that no one could object to the documents because so few people actually understood them. For example, instead of saying that the company was going to fire people without notice in order to save money on health insurance premiums, we would say that they were "engaging in reconstructive human resource strategies to build synergies in forward-looking ventures." We developed an expertise in drafting legal documents using neutral and formal terms that completely obscured the actual power relations at play between the parties. Obfuscation reaches new heights in the field of corporate law. Consider the embarrassment felt by former SEC Chairman Arthur Levitt when, as a condition of accepting the post, he was required to move his holdings into mutual funds: "As I pored over fund prospectuses, what really got under my skin was that the documents were impossible to understand. At first I was embarrassed. Then it hit me: if someone with twenty-five years in the securities business couldn't decipher the jargon, imagine the frustration of the average investor. Mutual fund prospectuses were written in impenetrable legalese, by and for securities lawyers."[29] Think about this "impenetrable legalese" the next time you are asked to sign a standard form contract at a rental car counter in an airport—the contract was undoubtedly designed by corporate lawyers so you won't realize how many rights you've signed away. And most of this backroom work by corporate lawyers is invisible, since the blame falls on the *client*. Almost everyone can name a brutish corporation or two, but almost no one can name a nasty law firm. Only when the entire corporate system was challenged in the wake of the Enron collapse did a few senators finally wake up and realize that lawyers were "at the scene of the crime" and that "in almost every transaction there was a lawyer who drew up the documents."[30]

When I practiced corporate law, I felt insulated from critique because the work that I was doing was so complex that virtually no one had the ability to challenge it; indeed, only one person in ten thousand could have deciphered the documents I was drafting, and those few people would be my peers and colleagues. A recent article in *American Lawyer* describes one such complex deal that was cooked up at a big firm:

An investor forms a single-member limited liability company. The LLC borrows money from an investment bank, then uses that money to buy a long option from the bank and sell a short option to the bank. The net cost to the investor is minimal. A general partnership is created. The LLC becomes a general partner, and contributes the option positions and minimal capital assets. The investor's basis is inflated because he or she claims basis from the contribution of the long position but no reduction in basis from the short position. An S corporation is created. The LLC contributes its interest in the general partnership to the S corporation in exchange for stock. The partnership terminates. The options expire. The S corporation's assets are then sold, triggering a capital loss that passes through to the investor.[31]

This makes sense only if you are willing to totally bracket all ethical, social, and political effects of your work and instead view the law as a giant game to be manipulated so that your client can avoid taxes. This is the attitude of most young corporate lawyers. Consider the description of "A Day in the Life of a Corporate Law Associate" posted on the Vault website, a popular discussion forum for young lawyers, keeping in mind that this was provided in all seriousness and without a shred of irony:

9:30:   Arrive at work. Check e-mail and voice-mail.

10:00:   You are performing due diligence in connection with a sale by a large realty group. ("Basically I'm spending my time making sure all the documents have been delivered as well as dotting the i's and crossing the t's").

12:30:   Break for lunch at the firm's cafeteria. ("They have everything in the cafeteria. There's pizza everyday, gourmet entrees . . . ").

2:00:   On a separate deal that you are working on—a $75 million acquisition—you are drafting parts of documents. ("As a second year, I don't necessarily draft an entire document, but I'll draft provisions.")

3:00:   You call co-counsel to discuss one of the provisions you are drafting. Although you feel that this provision is relatively minor he is very concerned about it. The discussion lasts over an hour.

5:30:   You have a question relating to the discussion you had with co-counsel as well as another provision of the contract, so you discuss it with the partner assigned to the deal ("The partners are approachable here. You can talk to them—and they will have no problem talking to you.")

8:30:   You continue working on drafting parts of the document, breaking to order Indian food.

10:00:   You call the car service and go home.[32]

This appears to be a day without *content*. There is no indication of what is being done, why it is being done, and for whom. The social world, indeed the *external* world, has dropped out of the picture.

Several years into my tenure with a large firm, I realized that I was gaining weight, drinking to calm my nerves, and spending all my time at the firm. The real legal work didn't begin until the daytime staff went home at 5:00 P.M. and the office was sufficiently quiet to begin the drafting process, so I generally ate all of my meals at work. And the closer I looked at the partners, the more scared I became. Many of them had lost connection to their children and spouses, they had few passionate interests, and hardly ever read books. In the law firm's biography section, many of these men had listed their hobbies as bird watching and golf, two nondescript and harmless pastimes. There was not a single genuine offbeat character in the group. They were hyper-educated with degrees from Ivy League schools, but as far as I could determine they had no insights into their own behavior and were completely incapable of sustaining an intellectual discussion about the morality of our legal practice.

Not long after I quit the large firm, two authors of a study on corporate lawyers came to my alma mater, Northwestern University Law School, and told the students, "After five, ten, or fifteen years of practicing law, you will loathe practicing law. You will wake up in the morning and hate to go to work."[33] While this is not true of every lawyer at every firm, it is the reality of too many lawyers at too many firms. In fact, law professor Patrick Schiltz traveled the country in support of a seminal article on lawyer unhappiness, and in each city he would challenge audience members to name one big-firm partner who lives a balanced life and is also considered a success by his partners: he is still waiting for an answer.[34]

If you ask big-firm lawyers about the moral, social, and political implications of representing large institutions at the expense of weaker parties, they will fall back on the adversary system excuse and the free market: "Everyone deserves representation," they will say, "and we are simply lucky enough to represent the best-paying clients. In a free-market system, any person or institution can hire a lawyer if they are willing to pay."

But I never bought into that. Despite being trained to "think like a lawyer," I could not see any honor in being a cog within a corrupt and unbalanced system where the powerful use the law as a blunt instrument to crush the weak. Appeals to the "adversary system" and the "free market" are only as good as the adversary system and the free market, and my experience told me that they didn't work very well. Law should be an instrument for making the world better—it should not magnify the injustices that already exist. This is why I can never understand why there is so much prestige in working at a large law firm. At the end of the day, you are simply delaying lawsuits, forcing people into unfair contracts, helping the rich avoid taxation, and making life miserable for workers and consumers. That's no way for a young person to live.

chapter six:
Technology and the Overwrought Lawyer

John Stuart Mill once observed, "It is questionable if all the mechanical inventions yet made have lightened the day's toil of any human being."[1] A similar question might be raised about the myriad technological devices that are now *de rigueur* for even the most pedestrian law office. Today's fully automated law firm is a marvel of modern machinery, outfitted with computers, wireless networking, voice mail, e-mail, fax machines, Federal Express, pagers, cell phones, copiers, scanners, shredders, virtual conferencing, Web portals, deal rooms, document management systems, and sophisticated software programs that chart every action, every expense, every phone call, every copy, and every billable moment in every day. But has this orgy of technology brought us happiness? Has it made the practice of law better, or easier? Wasn't that the point of all this stuff in the first place? Like many lawyers, I suspect that the recent advances in technology have made the practice of law more difficult, and while this is not the principal source of unhappiness for young lawyers, it definitely contributes to the elevated demands placed on them.

To take a single example, I would suggest that the fax machine causes more problems than it solves for most lawyers. True, there are times that you need a document right away, and the facsimile machine is a godsend. But I have seen lawyers driven to near madness by this commonplace device. In a high-pressure law office where I used to work, there was a very successful fifth-year associate who suffered the extreme misfortune of being assigned the office closest to the "fax room." Every time a bell went off announcing an incoming fax, the associate would stiffen in his chair and a look of misery would flash across his face, much like a dog that knows through hard experience that a punishment is sure to follow a high-pitched sound. After noticing this physical transformation occur several times a day for weeks on end, I ventured into his office and asked him why he reacted so strongly to the fax machine. I will never forget his response:

> I became a lawyer to have independence and control over my work, but I've become a slave to the fax machine. It ruins my life. I send something out to a client, go to the bathroom to pee, and by the time I get back, the document has returned with changes. I send out a redlined version and it comes back again—the document is never finished. I might as well be chained to the fax machine. I have degrees from Princeton and Harvard so I could work in a civilized profession, not to be enslaved to a machine like a factory worker. I'd love to smash it to bits.

Was this man crazy? Hardly. He was perfectly sane. In fact, he had inadvertently put his finger on what I would like to call the *Paradox of Technology*, which is that many recent inventions promising to save time for attorneys actually have the unintended effect of consuming additional time. More accurately, technological inventions create new tasks and raise expectations, thereby canceling out the time they save. So even if the fax machine were to be totally replaced by e-mail attachments or imaging technology that converted documents to "pdf" format, this would save time in the short term but would raise a fresh set of technological frustrations and elevated expectations that would eat up the time savings and force lawyers to work even harder. With regard to the practice of law, this much is painfully clear: the law office of the new century is full of timesaving devices, yet we are working harder than ever. It sounds bizarre, but perhaps if we had fewer timesaving devices, we might spend less time at the office.

Most rational people accept the basic fact that technology is inevitable, that it cannot be obliterated, and that we cannot turn back time. But if lawyers cannot go back to a golden age (assuming it ever existed), then perhaps we *can* make some minor changes to make our lives more balanced and more humane. In this chapter I want to explore how technology has changed the practice of law, and I will recommend that lawyers reconsider how they presently use technology in their practice. As a frame of reference, please keep in mind that recent empirical evidence has not been able to establish any sort of link between profitability and the use of cutting-edge legal technology. As the *American Lawyer* technology supplement flatly declared, "The reality is that the most profitable firms are profitable for reasons having little or nothing to do with technology."[2] In fact, some of the most profitable firms in America are the *least* advanced technologically.

The Paradox of Technology

Earlier I alluded to what I called the *Paradox of Technology*, which is that the technological apparatuses designed to save time actually consume time. The irony of this phenomenon was not lost on Sigmund Freud, who explored the question of whether advances in technology would bring happiness to people:

> One would like to ask: is there no positive gain in pleasure, no unequivocal increase in my feeling of happiness, if I can, as often as I please, hear the voice of a child of mine who is living hundreds of miles away or if I can learn in the shortest possible time after a friend has reached his destination that he has come through a long and difficult voyage unharmed? But here the voice of pessimistic criticism makes itself heard. If there had been no railway to conquer distances, my child would never have left his native town and I should need no telephone to hear his voice; if traveling across the ocean by ship had not been introduced, my friend would not have embarked on his sea-voyage and I should not need a cable to relieve my anxiety about him.[3]

Freud makes the point that technology seems to bring people together, yet at the same time it separates them; it provides a cure, but it creates the disease. For example, the advent of railways make it easier to visit one's relatives in a distant part of the country, but the relatives probably would not be living so far away in the first place if the railway had not taken them there. So the railway *solves* the problem of distance, but it was partially responsible for *creating* this problem. This results in a net wash.

A similar point was also made by the well-respected sociologist Thorstein Veblen in the early part of the twentieth century, when he raised the scandalous question of whether the typewriter actually saves time. Veblen said that at first blush the typewriter seems to save time because it allows more documents to be produced in comparison with handwriting. But there is a catch: by making it easier to produce documents, the typewriter places a higher volume of letters, documents, and junk mail into circulation, so that the volume of correspondence blows up beyond all actual need and necessity, thereby wasting our time.[4]

Both of these thinkers drew attention to a little-noticed fact about technology—that each new device raises our expectations, and once raised, our expectations are rarely lowered. Here is an example to which most lawyers can relate: the client wants a document *now*, not because he really needs it now, but because he can get it now. In a world of quicker/faster/stronger/open all night, the production of law is no different from consumer goods: the customer wants everything now or he will take his business to someone else. As a result, lawyers are forced to produce documents immediately and send everything by fax, FedEx, or e-mail attachment, creating the impression of efficiency, even when there is no real need to have the documents delivered so quickly.

The recent advancements in computerized legal research have also raised the bar on what is expected of lawyers, nullifying the gain achieved. It is true that *Lexis* and *Westlaw* allow a young lawyer to do all of her research in one place, making it possible to produce a legal brief in record time. This shortens the time-frame expectations of clients and increases the quality and quantity expectations of law firm partners. Long gone is the time-honored practice of walking among the stacks of court reporters, thinking about the case, holding the actual reporters in your hands and getting a physical feel for the weight of the law in your hands, rubbing shoulders with other lawyers. Now the law is reduced to words on a screen, cases from the year 1900 look identical to cases from the year 2000, and anyone can pull up twenty cases on any point simply by entering a few keywords. Since the law is an adversarial profession, this technology is used by both sides, and each side is forced to counteract the other's use of technology, much like two neighbors armed with snow blowers who are continually shifting massive loads of snow back and forth on each other's driveways. Although there are undeniable conveniences to having the ability to do legal research at night on a home computer, or to file a bankruptcy petition by e-mail, the result is a net wash due to the general overproduction of unnecessary and repetitive legal briefs containing excessive citations. Here, as elsewhere, the technology has not made the practice of law any easier.

If you are an attorney over the age of thirty-five, you probably look back with some fondness on the ancient days when each client had a "file" which contained all of the relevant information in one central location. Back then, every note and every document involving the client was placed in this file. Those days are long gone. While there is still a file for every client in what might be called "hard copy" (that is, paper), there are now additional bits and pieces of information floating around in several different formats. For example, there may be e-mail messages about the matter that are not in the file, voice-mail messages that were never written down and placed in the file, notes and phone messages floating around in computer files, drafts of letters sitting in cyberspace, and so on. The spreading of information across so many different formats gives rise to tremendous confusion, often between people who work in the same office and who could easily communicate more efficiently in person.

Consider the following scenario, which is not uncommon nowadays within a single firm: the lawyer in office A sends a voice-mail message to the lawyer in office B to the effect that they need to talk about client C. Attorney B responds with an e-mail message to lawyer A, who has meanwhile left B a handwritten note. These attorneys have still not connected, so A decides to send B a message in the "Notes" library of the client's WordPerfect subfile, while B awaits word from A by scanning the message section of Day-Timer. Meanwhile, client C calls and the message is placed by a secretary in the phone log database, where it is ignored by both lawyers. All of these messages are placed in different formats, in what might be called different "dimensions" (paper, WordPerfect, voice-mail, e-mail, and Day-Timer). How is it possible to stay abreast of every dimension? Only by remaining isolated in an office, surrounded by a computer, voice mail, and e-mail, busily scanning every port of entry for the latest missive to arrive. Nobody knows when the next message will arrive or what format it will arrive in, but there is always a gnawing fear that it will be stored where nobody can find it.

The irony in all of this is that the very technology that promised to bring us closer together has driven us farther apart. In the prior era, attorneys were forced to communicate in person or through the ancient art of writing messages using paper and pen. But this practice, which worked well for hundreds of years, is slowly giving way to the use of computers to store all information. As a result, law has become less of a collegial profession, since each office becomes a miniature law firm, replete with its own computer terminal, printer, and phone message system.

An important aspect of the new telecommunications technology is that it allows for increased mobility—so a lawyer can be "connected" to the office and "reachable" even if she is not physically present. But here again the benefits may be outweighed by the disadvantages. Lawyers who remain constantly connected to the workplace by cell phone, fax, and e-mail sometimes feel, justifiably, that a cloud is hanging over their heads. On the one hand, there are obvious advantages in being connected to the workplace, since it allows an attorney to be consulted at any time of the day to lend advice to ongoing projects. But on the other hand, this connection can be horribly intrusive. Consider, for example, the attorney who leaves the office but stays connected by cell phone, pager, call-forwarding, or laptop computer. The existence of these connecting devices ensures that the attorney is never totally free, never in a nonwork space. Because of the new technology, the line between workplace and nonworkplace diminishes to the vanishing point, where the lawyer often cannot tell whether he is really at work or not, since he occupies a sort of netherworld between work/leisure and office/home. The very devices that allow the attorney to take time out of the office are what connect him to the office like an invisible umbilical cord. As a result, there really is no chance to get *away* completely from work: it is as if the attorney is living in a walled city. This lends a certain claustrophobic quality to the practice of law. The feeling is so pervasive that an attorney friend of mine recently took me aside and confessed to the mortal sin of turning off his cell phone at times, saying "There are times when I don't want to be reached." This perfectly normal reaction was not looked upon favorably by his employer.

It might be noted that a similar effect has taken place throughout society as a whole. Consider the famous French artist Paul Gauguin, who traveled from France to the South Sea Islands in 1891. Try to imagine, if you will, the conceptual change occasioned by such a move, what a totally different way of life he encountered. We can really say that Gauguin truly got away to a different dimension of experience. Now we might wonder what would happen if Gauguin tried to make the same trip today. The picture is less romantic: no doubt he would be sitting at the beach, "connected" by Internet, e-mail, phone, fax, and Federal Express, watching HBO, CNN, and Court TV. Just as there is no longer an "outside" to Europe and America because there is now an international culture of television, pop music, and Coca-Cola, there is no longer an outside to the workplace: one is always either at work or, to use the modern parlance, "reachable." But isn't it possible that there is a human downside, an emotional cost to being reachable?

The loss of any boundary between work and leisure was clearly illustrated when the *Wall Street Journal* profiled the vacation agenda of a chief executive officer: "By dinner time, he has fielded 17 business calls and phoned five important clients. He also receives a special delivery of 'must-read' work papers, 18 faxes, and 27 e-mail messages."[5] Says another CEO (somewhat oblivious to contradiction): "I'm working all the time when I'm on vacation." According to a study by Pitney Bowes (the maker of postage meters), the *average* person receives 32 phone calls, 11 voice mails, 9 faxes, 6 post-it notes, and 5 telephone message slips in a given day.[6] Interestingly, the study found that these different media for information are not replacing each other (for example, a fax message being sent instead of a phone call, or an e-mail message instead of a fax), but rather that these messages are layered over each other, creating five or six levels of information. According to one executive, "A plane ride is no longer a time to work quietly or read a trashy novel. It's time to be scheduled and invaded"; another executive concludes that "there is no line between work and home. I put my pager next to my bed . . . I have to."[7] The important thing to note here is the sense of resignation and submission among these very successful people who give the appearance of being in complete control of their lives, as if there were nothing that they could do to avoid the invasive technology. Of course, there is always the fear that if one turns off the cell phone (even for a little while), clients will flee, the competitive edge will be lost, and financial ruin will result.

The Virtual Law Office, Awash in Paper

Technology is advancing at such a rate that the very concept of the "law office" may become outdated. In an era of profits over people, it is inevitable that somebody begins to wonder whether it is cost effective for each attorney (especially associates) to have a separate office when the basic lawyering tasks can be done "on the road," as it were. Sound unlikely? Well, consider that the *Wall Street Journal* published an article a few years ago on the "Virtual Office," which is techno-speak for "No Office."[8] The article profiled a series of workers who had been relieved of their offices and were now performing the same tasks at home (or wandering the highways and byways), armed with cell phones, laptop computers, scanners, and portable fax machines—everything but the actual office itself. Several accounting firms have made the move to a virtual office system, and law firms could be next.[9] One Michigan CPA firm "exists only in cyberspace," and its founders are justifiably worried about a "sense of isolation and a loss of team spirit."[10]

This disturbing scenario is perhaps less frightening than a similar negative utopia which was played out recently in the pages of *Inc. Magazine*, which profiled a man who ran his company out of his Lexus. The car was fully loaded with a computer, fax machine, phone, and other high-tech gadgets. According to this man, who somehow manages to drive his car amid the distractions of running a business from the driver's seat, "The office of the 1990s has four *wheels*, not four *walls*." Amazingly, one of the magazine's pundits felt that this Orwellian set-up did not go far enough because the man lacked a PowerBook and a portable shredder: "By itself, a car with a fax, a notebook computer, and a cellular phone is just a gadget-filled car, not a *mobile office*."[11] If this trend reaches the practice of law, we may be witnessing the end of the law office (at least, for associates), and the rise of a flex-office, perhaps in the form of a general office area outfitted with movable carrels, available on a day-by-day basis for those lawyers who need a home base for a few hours. The bottom line is that privacy costs money, so the private law office may be one of the first casualties in the push among law firms for greater profits. I don't mean to depress you, but try to picture what it would be like to work as a flex-time associate with no benefits, operating out of a virtual office that you carry around in your briefcase like some sort of secret agent in a B-movie.

One way to measure whether technology has helped the practice of law is to compare how things stood before and after the introduction of a particular piece of technology. Let's begin with the most important piece of technology for the law office, the computer. The beauty of the computer (versus the typewriter) is that it allows documents to be revised onscreen and then stored as a form for future legal work. One would think that the computer must be a blessing for the legal profession, that it has improved our lives immensely because documents can be drafted from previous documents, thus shortening the preparation time. But is this really the case? If you ask lawyers who have practiced for a long time they will tell you that, strangely enough, things were easier before each lawyer had a computer in his office. How can this be?

For one thing, prior to the use of computers, lawyers used shorter documents, and in addition, they relied more heavily on forms that needed to be typed. Lawyers knew that it was physically impossible to type every possible provision into a document, so they made the document the best that it could be under the circumstances, and then sent it to the client by regular mail. The client received the document a few days later, and, knowing that wide-scale revision would be cumbersome, requested minor adjustments and basically used the document as drafted. A lawyer recently told me that in the 1960s, the turnaround time for a corporate document (say, an employment agreement, lease, or shareholder agreement) was ten days to two weeks. Nowadays clients expect to see something overnight.

Notice how the technology of that era placed a limit on what lawyers could accomplish, thereby ensuring that things could not be done at a pace or on a scale that outstretched human endurance. Put simply, since the document could not be fifty pages long, nobody tried to make it that long. And since the document took several days to reach the client, there was time for a breathing space between revisions, which meant that there was a period during which nothing more could be done, when the lawyer could rest. To be sure, lawyers worked very hard in those days, but there was a technological limit to what they could achieve, and this limit kept the practice on a more human scale.

With the dawn of the computer, it became quite easy to push a button and crank out a long document, replete with exhibits. My guess is that, at first blush, clients were impressed with the newer, longer documents, because for all they knew, the lawyer drafted the documents from scratch. But once it dawned on the clients that lawyers could crank out the documents at the push of a button, the clients had the reverse reaction—now they suspected that the lawyer had done very little work, and that the real work lay ahead, in revising the documents. After all, if a document is sitting in the computer just waiting to be revised, why not put it through another draft? One result of this is that lawyers anticipate that a document will be put through endless drafts, so they begin by sending out a rough draft, with the idea that it could be revised time and again. When this happens, many drafts and redlined versions are sent back and forth, which hardly seems like an improvement in efficiency.

Now when we complete this picture by considering the use of e-mail attachment and fax as a way for the client to send his revisions back to the lawyer immediately, the verdict is inescapable—the computer not only does not save time, but in fact makes the process of lawyering a never-ending task, because there is no technological endpoint to the drafting process, which now extends to the very last second before the document is signed. I have belabored this point slightly, but it should come as no revelation to any attorney who has spent an entire afternoon faxing a document back and forth to a client for countless revisions (with the inevitable calls that "I didn't receive page 3," or "Page 5 came out blurry") or who has spent an afternoon trying to figure out which e-mail attachment is the latest of the dozen versions that have been sent back and forth.

But if the computer does not really save time, perhaps it has other advantages. One promise of the computer age was that lawyers would eventually use less paper, because communication, negotiations, and the revision of documents would take place online or be stored on disks. The idea is that we would use paper only when it was time to print out a *final* document, thus eliminating hard copies of drafts, unsightly cutting-and-pasting, and the use of corrective fluid ("white-out"). How well has this prediction panned out?

As for the claim that we will no longer use white-out, I can report that my hands were recently stained with white-out from making last-second changes to a Stock Purchase Agreement that was already heavily revised by both sets of attorneys and their clients. As for cutting-and-pasting, it has gone high-tech: a company is now marketing a cut-and-paste apparatus for lawyers that allows inserts to be typed on a clear background so that they can be pasted onto documents without giving the appearance of having been pasted. This venerable tradition, then, continues.

But what about the ideal of a paperless society? An article appeared in the 1980s in *Crain's Chicago Business*, in which a well-known business columnist predicted that the widespread use of computers would lead to a paperless society. He envisioned a world where everybody was connected by computers and telephones so there would be no need to communicate by paper. This prediction was put to the test as law offices became fully computerized. Once the evidence was in, the columnist retracted his prediction and instead flatly admitted that he was completely wrong—computers were not saving paper, but were in fact churning out more paper than we previously used:

> I hereby retract the whole [prediction]. Let's face it, all of us are drowning in paper. And what is the cause of this new flood of paper? It's obvious. The technological marvels that were supposed to remove paper from our lives are spewing it out at such a ridiculous rate that I fear for the tree population of North America. . . . If you don't believe me, then consider some of the whizbang hardware that you undoubtedly have in your shop, [like] the computer. Rather than cut down on paper, this monster generates a blizzard of paper.[12]

The same conclusion was reached by the author of a column on law office management:

> For lawyers, at least, the idea of the paperless office turned out to be a cruel joke. As computers were utilized more broadly, the flow of paper increased instead of lessening. Briefs became less brief. A thirty-page document was as easy to produce as a ten-page document. Numerous interrogatories became routine in even small cases. Fax machines allowed you to respond almost instantly instead of waiting for mail delivery. Today the average lawyer spends significantly more time and money on paper than ever before. . . . Many of us can recall when the entire court file in a divorce case might consist of five or six pages. Yet even in this Information Age, highly computerized law offices are still frequently shut down while everyone searches for a lost file, document, or phone number.[13]

Lawyers are simply not free to act spontaneously without leaving a paper trail. Just as Midas turned everything to gold, lawyers turn everything to paper and reduce the day to ten-minute segments in which they are writing down what they are doing. Every conversation requires a follow-up letter, every decision a confirmation, every step involves some sort of documentation, to the point where the lawyer seems to be swimming in paper and standing outside of himself with a stopwatch recording his time.

There is something disconcerting about being surrounded all day with paper entities like corporations, limited partnerships, trusts, and securities. One gets the creeping sense of existing in an artificial, made-up world. To be sure, a corporation is a real thing in the sense that it has an independent existence, but at the same time it is not a genuine person, something that one can connect with. The loss of reality hits home when a lawyer takes the time to do something in the real world, like paint her apartment—there is a sense that one has actually created something that makes a difference, instead of working for three hours to produce an opinion letter so carefully worded that it says nothing.

Almost every lawyer can identify with the sensation of having spent all day preparing the most abstract and ephemeral documents, only to come home from work and get a hug and a kiss that sends a bizarre shock through the body. It is not a pleasurable feeling, really, but more a jolt—a reminder that there is flesh and bone in the world, that something is more real than the corporations and limited partnerships that one is working with from early morning to late night. That shock that the lawyer feels on direct contact with others speaks volumes about the way that legal work separates the lawyer from human relationships and surrounds him in a paper world.

With regard to the needless proliferation of paper, you might want to conduct the following simple experiment: go to a major law firm and look at the binders that hold the closing documents for corporate or real estate transactions, and compare the binders for deals that closed before 1970 with recent transactions of the same relative size and complexity. You will find that a very large transaction in the 1970s was documented in one medium-size binder, whereas a similar transaction from 2004 fills four or five large binders. Is all this additional paper really necessary? Why do we need so much more paper to close a deal? One would think that if we were moving toward increasing technology, we could get more information in less space, just as our cars and computers and watches have gotten smaller.

Part of the problem here is the general overproduction of law, which is evidenced by the growth in statutory law and administrative regulations. By way of example, consider the Illinois statutes: in 1901 the Illinois Revised Statutes were collected in one volume, the 1971 Statutes took up three volumes, the 1992 Statutes fill six volumes, and so on. In other words, it seems that statutory law doubles in size every twenty years. One would expect that this would make the practice of law easier, that the law would now be clearer and more exact. But, paradoxically, the reverse has occurred. There are now innumerable rules to comply with and endless forms to submit for every transaction and lawsuit. The simplest matter easily turns into a complicated research project. Guido Calabresi has famously commented that American law is "choking on statutes,"[14] which removes the law further from its common law basis in general principles, but also has the effect of making the law so complex that each lawyer can understand only a small corner of the whole. This effectively incapacitates a lawyer from practicing in multiple areas because the learning curve is too steep; her only recourse is to stay within her little area and, paradoxically, to make her area even more complex, as a way of protecting it from intruders and guaranteeing herself a market. This was clearly evidenced in the recent revisions of Article 9 of the Uniform Commercial Code, which is now nearly three times longer than the previous Article 9, and can be understood by only a few lawyers in the entire country— namely the people who drafted it.[15]

This level of complexity has the result of turning the law into a private language instead of a public discourse, thereby creating public distrust and a growing sense that lawyers are enacting complicated laws simply to generate demand for their own services. When the law becomes encyclopedic with statutes and regulations, it loses the ability to inspire and becomes so technical that it cannot be used as a guide for ordinary citizens. In this way, legal language separates ordinary citizens from the law and causes them to feel alienated and bitter toward lawyers. When the greatest legal philosopher of the twentieth century, H.L.A. Hart, raised the question of what a *pathological* legal system would look like, he concluded that it would be one dominated by a small group of insiders who could grasp the law while the mass of people couldn't understand the law but were required to obey it nonetheless.[16] Amazingly, that is precisely the condition toward which we are descending.

This hypercomplexity reaches a breaking point when lawyers themselves are completely clueless on how to comply with the law. When former President Clinton sought to nominate Zoe Baird as Attorney General, her candidacy was derailed by a failure to comply with the rules of taxation and immigration for her babysitter. Soon thereafter, a book about hyper-regulation, entitled *The Death of Common Sense,* appeared on the *New York Times* bestseller list; the author (himself an attorney) asked a poignant question, "When law is too dense to be known, too detailed to be sensible, and is always tripping us up, why should we respect it?"[17] The problem here is not merely that the law has become tedious and boring, or that lawyers no longer have basic principles of law to hang their hats upon, but rather that the law has become fragmented and complex to the point that even the people on the inside have lost sight of the system as a whole. The result is a Frankenstein monster of laws and regulations, one that threatens our ideal of populist democracy. After all, the democratic ideal is that citizens are *consensually* bound by laws that they have approved through their elected representatives. The moral force of the law rests heavily on the pillars of equal access to law and due notice of law for all citizens. This ideal is threatened when the mass of citizens cannot begin to understand the legal system or the documents that control their lives.[18] When taken to an extreme, the situation becomes that described by Kafka in his short parable *The Problem of Our Laws*, in which a group of nobles refuses to let the public see the law, so a segment of the population comes to believe that there is no law at all and that the whole thing is a farce concocted by the nobles to keep the people subservient.[19] In fact, Supreme Court Justice Anthony Kennedy said that all lawyers and law students must read Kafka's novel *The Trial* because it captures the reality of law for most Americans.[20] Here we have a member of the Supreme Court saying that the legal system is best captured by a novel about a man who is arrested and ultimately executed without being advised of the charges against him and without getting to appear before a court, and who spends the entire novel shifting among useless lawyers and functionaries who inform him that the law is totally unfathomable.

The former dean of Stanford Law School, Bayless Manning, has termed our condition *hyperlexis*: "the pathological condition of an overactive law-making gland."[21] Manning was particularly outraged when the Treasury Department issued 110 single-spaced pages of regulations to *clarify* the distinction between "debt" and "equity" under Section 385 of the Tax Code. As Manning complained,

> The law must rely fundamentally on the voluntary compliance of the citizenry. The legal system of a democratic society cannot operate—and that means that a democratic society cannot operate—if the law is allowed to become so elaborate that it is beyond the reach of the informed, literate citizen who would like to be law-abiding. . . . Regulation has become so elaborate and technical that it is beyond the understanding of all but a handful of Mandarins, [and] only the largest enterprises can afford to pay for the professional help that is required to pick one's way through the thicket. . . . If we let that happen to our law, the people of the United States are simply going to say "To hell with it."[22]

In other words, the rule of law disappears in a fragmentary and impenetrable web of regulations propagated by federal and state administrative agencies, municipalities, commissions, and other bodies. A set of regulations so diffuse and piecemeal cannot command respect or legitimacy because nobody can be put on notice of it in advance, and because so few people can understand it. Ordinary people begin to view the legal system as if it were some type of impossible code imposed by aliens from outer space.

Even the officials inside the system (that is, judges and lawyers) have only a small glimpse of certain pieces of the whole, because the whole has grown baffling, unfathomable, like the infinite Library of Babel in Borges's fable.[23] Therein lies the pathology—the law is so complex and overregulated that even to those on the inside, it often seems arbitrary and groundless. Even a general lawyer cannot give advice to a client on a simple matter such as a breach of contract or a simple negligence claim, unless and until the lawyer carefully scours the statutes and rules of court; after all, there are special rules for every type of contract. When the law is so complicated, lawyers are put in constant fear of malpractice.

Brevity and succinctness mark the documents that continue to inspire successive generations of Americans, documents such as the Declaration of Independence and the Constitution. To be sure, rough edges and ambiguities abound in the Constitution (what exactly is "due process?"), but it is short enough to be understood as a whole, as a document with clear purpose and design, something that the individual citizen can affirm as his own. We cannot compare this sentiment with the feeling engendered by staring at ten thousand pages of single-spaced EPA regulations. What is lost is precisely the experience of seeing oneself reflected in the laws made by one's officials, which is essential to democracy. To be sure, any society as complex as ours will need a complex legal system. Yet as I have documented, there is a wide-spread sentiment that the legal system is out of control, like a monster that no longer heeds the call of its master. If we continue our present course, we are headed toward a legal system of mystifying complexity, administered by a select group of insiders who know only a small corner of the system, sur-rounded by an expanding ring of outsiders who are growing increasingly frustrated. As the law gets more complex and the young lawyer finds himself inside this monster, he becomes increasingly alienated from nonlawyers and unable to explain to them precisely what he is doing and why.

Record Keeping ad Nauseam

Much of the new technology for the law office, especially the new time-and-billing software programs, were designed with the goal of monitoring the minutiae of every day, which is theoretically possible, but pragmatically absurd. As the result of this technology, lawyers have developed a kind of hyperattention to timekeeping and expenses, such that every second of the day and every movement must be accounted for, invoiced, and documented; the most innocent conversation gives rise to feelings that one is wasting time, and the impetus toward efficiency is taken to surreal heights. The result is a Panopticon, a type of prison where the inmates can be watched and yet never know whether they are being monitored.

The new time-and-billing software was supposed to make billing more accurate, since it ostensibly allows the lawyer to assign every action and ex-pense to a particular client, so no time is free-floating and wasted. This cre-ates an incentive for lawyers to write down every task that they perform. The problem, however, is that no sane person can do this, or rather, that the en-tire process seems to have reached a point of absurdity. To see my point, let's ask ourselves whether the highly technological, computer-driven programs are really an improvement over the previous methods of billing.

If you examine legal bills from the 1950s and 1960s, you'll be shocked by the amazing lack of information, primarily because most projects were billed at a set fee according to fee schedules or customary prices. For exam-ple, a standard contract might cost $100 as a base rate, which the lawyer could raise depending on the situation. This is sometimes referred to as "proj-ect billing" in order to distinguish it from the current practice of "hourly billing." In old legal bills, it was customary to give a very brief description, such as "For Legal Services Rendered in Connection with XYZ Matter: $1,000.00." This one-sentence bill (let's call it "Bill 1") contrasts sharply with the modern bill, which can run for dozens of pages containing hundreds of entries, each covering a time frame as small as ten minutes:

> Call from client to discuss summons and complaint (.3); receive fax from client (.1, no charge, expense $10); call back to client to discuss counts I and II (.5); have associate retrieve annotated statute on motion to dismiss (.2); call to attorney Smith for plaintiff, not available, left message (.2); conference with Partner X (.3); strategy meeting with Able, Block, and Carter (.8); call to client re: insurance (.2); call to docket department to docket case (.2); read Jones case (.3) and Shepard's for same (.1).

Let's call this "Bill 2." Now, which of these bills is better for the practice of law, Bill 1 or Bill 2?

Bill 1 takes much less time to prepare, so it frees the lawyer from time that he would otherwise spend preparing the bill itself. To be sure, it represents a sort of rough figure, rounded off, so it is not entirely accurate to the last penny. But if the client calls up to complain, the bill can be negotiated, reexamined, and adjusted.

The ostensible advantage of Bill 2 is that it can be pulled up from an electronic billing system with the touch of a button. But in actuality what gets pulled up is an unedited and haphazard compilation of entries from various people at various times, with no sense of the whole bill. So a "billing attorney" must now spend a tremendous amount of unbillable time getting the bill presentable for the client, a process that (it's no secret) involves the creative recharacterization of various tasks so that they sound better. Entries like "Spoke with partner X about the lawsuit" must be revised to "Strategy meeting for aggressive responsive pleading." And since this takes place days or weeks after the events, the process involves a high degree of fiction and historical revisionism. The practice of padding and rewriting history is so common that we can empathize with Webb Hubbell, the former associate attorney general (and friend of the Clintons) who was jailed for overbilling while in private practice: when his wife asked whether it was true that he overbilled clients, he said, "Yes, I did. So does every lawyer in the country."[24] This hardly excuses his conduct, but he is basically correct in that the problem touches most lawyers.

The problem here is that the goal of the billing software—to measure every minute of every day—is physically impossible for most human beings. Spending one's time reconstructing the day into little six-minute segments is a challenging experiment for students in Psychology 101, but it hardly seems like something that a grown person should be doing day in and day out. To top it off, the process cannot really be done with any degree of accuracy. The idea was that clients would benefit by seeing how the lawyers spent every millisecond. But since nobody really spends all of their time so efficiently, there is a huge amount of fudging going on, from the lawyer who pads the bill and rewrites history, to the billing partner who rewrites the bill to be more palatable. Yet amazingly, the industry trend is for lawyers to divide their time even further, into *three-minute* segments.[25] The whole thing is absurd.

How does the client see things? The client would seem better off receiving Bill 2, which details what the lawyer is doing at every possible moment, down to one-tenth of any hour. But not so fast—Bill 2 might provide too much information, which is often worse than no information at all. Does the client really need to know that the lawyer made a six-minute phone call to the Clerk of the Court, or that he spent twelve minutes talking to a partner about the case? Perhaps Bill 2 overwhelms the client with details, and it is easy to image the client picking up the bill and throwing it down in anger (something that is not too uncommon, I'm told).

A final observation: lawyers often solve problems by sitting and thinking for an extended period until a lightbulb goes off (so to speak), but the new software programs have no entries for this time-honored lawyer's practice. Forcing a lawyer to sit in front of the computer with a dictionary of "power words" to recharacterize her time may be an exercise in creativity, but this shows that the technology is not well adapted to what lawyers actually do, that lawyers are the ones adapting to the technology, not vice versa.

The rise of technology in the legal workplace also produces a new and strange behavior that I call the "billing reflex," a psychological condition that causes an attorney to write down what he is doing while he is actually doing it. For example, while the attorney is talking to the client, he is also writing down that he is talking to the client so that he doesn't forget to bill it. This is much the same as having a conversation with yourself in your head while talking to another person. Often this is done on the computer while talking to the client, because the newer software packages allow you to flip from one database to another. So when client X calls, one can switch from word processing to billing software, pull up the client's account, and turn on the "meter" so that the length of the conversation is recorded and billed. When a client calls a lawyer and hears her clicking away on the computer, she may be inclined to ask, "What is that clicking noise?" When the lawyer responds that he is entering notes and billing time on the computer, the client may feel that the lawyer is snubbing him, or that the lawyer is too busy to listen first and then write down the relevant facts later. In addition, the client may begin to feel like an impersonal number, a mere entry in the attorney's billing system.

The perils of timekeeping hang over every lawyer's life like a Sword of Damocles waiting to fall. It is difficult to explain to nonlawyers the contradictory pressures to bill the maximum number of hours (to appear productive) while avoiding overbilling (to appear efficient). There is a disturbing feeling in the pit of the stomach after a day of work when the time that you have billed doesn't quite measure out to the time you wanted to bill, or the time you thought you had entered throughout the day. At that moment a wave of fear passes through you, and you wish that you could conjure up more time through some sort of magical act. The entire billing system is so reviled by so many lawyers that one is shocked to find that most lawyers see it as an inevitable part of law, instead of a recent practice that is not set in stone.

The best-selling billing software for lawyers is Timeslips, which has a registered trademark declaring, "It turns time into money." Unbelievably, and perhaps ironically, the instruction manual is decorated with a painting of a man in a suit who is struggling to push a gigantic clock up a very steep hill. The image is fitting, since every day is a battle against the clock, which ticks away mercilessly like some kind of superpresence in the sky. Obsession with time is an occupational hazard of the profession.

One of the strange things about the new time-entry systems is that they allow anybody to check up on everybody else: everything that was once private is now potentially public. This lends a sort of Big Brother atmosphere to most firms, where each person is cautiously watching the other in a sort of Panopticon of mutual observation that transforms the work environment into a low-security, high-tech prison. Am I exaggerating? Ask yourself where else but a low-security prison would come up with the idea of putting access codes on copy machines, phones, and other services so that they can be accessed only after the client's number is punched into the keyboard. This phenomenon can make a lawyer feel tremendously guilty and look both ways before copying something for his personal use, such as an article from the newspaper that he found interesting.

Record keeping is doubtless essential for the practice of law, but it is gradually taking up more of the day's work. Record keeping is a tool, and we have surrounded ourselves with gadgets to make this easier, but it seems that the gadgets have taken over so that we begin to think like the gadgets themselves. As sociologist Lewis Mumford once explained:

> Time-keeping establishes a useful point of reference, and is invaluable for co-ordinating diverse groups and functions which lack any other common frame of activity. In the practice of an individual's vocation such regularity may greatly assist concentration and economize effort. But to make it arbitrarily rule over human functions is to reduce human existence itself to mere time-serving and to spread the shades of the prison house over too large an area of human conduct.[26]

Sometimes people come to resemble the machines that surround them. A friend of mine once worked at a law firm with a partner who ran his life like clockwork: every second was accounted for, every "i" was dotted and every "t" was crossed. My friend was admonished by the senior partner to watch this guy and to adopt his habits, because after all, he had the habits of a "highly effective person." One day a fellow associate told my friend that she had a conversation with this lawyer in which she confessed her frustrations about the profession. A curious thing happened at the end of the conversation: he told her that she had just "cost" him an hour of work, and that he would have to build this hour back into his schedule. She was understandably upset at having her conversation viewed as a quantitative "debit" on this man's schedule. It came to light two or three weeks later that the partner and his wife had adopted a child six months earlier and had not told anyone at the office—"It just didn't come up," this man said. Here was the guy that my friend was supposed to emulate—completely automated, a human machine. This is but a single example of a common occurrence in the field of law: powerful attorneys who wouldn't be tolerated in any other walk of life are somehow elevated as shining examples.

I suppose that we are moving toward a paradigm of law where each lawyer is an isolated individual, sitting alone in her office, facing a computer screen, surrounded by high-tech gadgets and piles and piles of papers stacked everywhere, interacting with others only through the screen. At the center of this storm is a human being, a social creature with a real need to connect with others, to feel their closeness and emotion. But this is becoming increasingly impossible, according to avant-garde social critic Jean Baudrillard:

> Just as the wolf-child becomes a wolf by living among them, so are we becoming functional. We are living the period of the objects: that is, we live by their rhythm, according to their incessant cycles. While objects are neither flora nor fauna, they give the impression of being a proliferating vegetation, a jungle whereby the new savage of modern times has trouble finding the reflexes of civilization. These flora and fauna, which people have produced, have come to circle and invest them, like a bad science-fiction novel.[27]

Baudrillard's point is that we are adapting to our objects, not vice versa—each person sits in a bubble, as it were, surrounded by his gizmos. This leads to a decline in what might be called "public space" where people can meet, since every relationship is mediated by technology, especially by computers. A foreshadowing of this phenomenon came to light several years ago when reports started to surface about Microsoft Chairman Bill Gates' cyber-dates with a woman from another town. First they spoke by cell phone, each saw a movie simultaneously in their own towns, and then they called each other after the movie to discuss it, each sitting with their own coffee.[28] Reflecting on this, Gates foresaw a brave new world of mediated relationships where people are connected by the Internet, but he failed to see how this creates a *Paradox of Technology* where these "connected" people are all sitting alone in their rooms.[29] The whole thing starts to resemble the science fiction nightmare sketched by E. M. Forster in *The Machine Stops*, depicting a future in which people live underground in isolated cells and communicate through screens, their lives run entirely by a giant central machine. In the practice of law, this negative utopia would be realized in a situation where each lawyer is an independent billing entity, spelling the death of the law firm as a cohesive unit, and the ascendency of the individual rainmaker as the prototypical lawyer, self-sufficient, a one-man firm with his own clients and his own technology, who need not link his fate with those who are less successful. In the future, it will be every man for himself, and the only link between lawyers will be the cash nexus.

Setting Limits

If I am correct, technology has not made the practice of law easier. Sure, it allows a young lawyer to send a draft contract to a client with the click of a button, but it inflames the expectations of clients and ultimately makes lawyers work longer and harder to produce the same results. For many lawyers, the boom in technology has transformed a civilized profession, so that lawyers now sit at their desks waiting to be bombarded by faxes, voice mail, e-mail, and overnight packages. Lawyers long for the end of the day, but it never really arrives, since the attorney is always connected and reachable. Ironically, as lawyers are increasingly connected to each other, they find themselves increasingly isolated. It is not unusual at times to sit at your desk and realize that in your workplace you are surrounded by objects instead of people, so that when somebody appears suddenly at your door and calls your name, you bolt upright as if shaken from a dream.

Technological inventions such as the fax machine were designed as tools for us to use. But we are getting the sense that the tools are using us, that the tool is the *subject* and we are the *object*, that we are slaves to the instruments we have created. Indeed, this is the underlying premise beneath much of the recent software for lawyers. Consider the American Bar Association's law office software *Amicus Attorney*, which sets the following tasks for 8:30–8:40 A.M., a *ten-minute period:*

> You arrive in the office and turn on your computer. After Windows fires up, you launch Amicus Attorney. First you examine your Daily Report, and scan to see the reminders of the appointments and deadlines you have scheduled for today. Then you enter the Calendar section and examine your To-Do's. You run through your To-Do's and look at the ranking of your items. While mentally going through the list, you recall something that you thought of yesterday evening and you create a new To-Do. After you assign your new entry a priority and link it to a file in your system, you reorder your list of To-Do's. While in your Calendar you also review your scheduled appointments. Scanning for free time, you note that your most recent

innovation, being a repeat appointment, from 8:30 to 8:40, has popped up on your calendar. This is an appointment that you have booked with yourself every morning at 8:30 to grab your cup of coffee, go through your appointments and schedule your day. As you scan your telephone messages that were recorded by your voice mail system last night, you schedule the time from 8:40 to 9:15 for returning these telephone calls plus those that you couldn't return from yesterday. Since your Amicus calendar is networked, your secretaries know that this time is meant for you to take calls but otherwise to be left undisturbed. You also copy your five most important To-Do entries and drag and drop them into your calendar. This creates appointments in your day for these entries. Moreover, you grab the mouse and drag the start and finish time bars for these entries until you are satisfied with the times allotted to each one in your day. You set alarms to go off when there is ten minutes left in each allotted time slot, to allow you to determine at that point to schedule for more time for these tasks or to finish up what you have done to that point in time and go on to other things. Having scheduled the five most important To-Do's in your day, you open your "Do Someday" list. This is your list of items that, while not pressing and urgent, are VERY important, such as taking time to market your practice or to think about your long-term personal and career goals. You examine your schedule and schedule a 15-minute appointment to take time to "sharpen the saw," in the words of Steven Covey.[30]

This is a classic example of an attempt to bend a profession into the shape of a computer program.

Many people will have trouble accepting my argument that technology has made the legal profession *worse*, because they are accustomed to thinking that technology is inherently *neutral* and therefore cannot make a profession better or worse. A position along these lines was articulated by philosopher Karl Jaspers when he said, "Technology is *per se* neither good nor evil, but it can be used for either good or evil."[31] This has intuitive appeal: after all, it would seem that any piece of technology (say, a hammer) can be used for good (building a house) or for evil (bashing someone's head in). This "technology is neutral" argument holds water for primitive technology, but it breaks down when we start to consider technological advancements such as electric chairs, napalm, computer viruses, laboratory anthrax, weapons of mass destruction, and the like. These are indeed instances of technology lacking any socially useful role; and they were not discovered in the scientist's search for truth but were instead specifically developed to achieve particular nefarious results. This means that we ought to drop the metaphor of technology as a neutral tool and instead see it as a way of viewing the world, a method of manipulation to achieve a specific goal.[32] In other words, someone started with a preconceived notion (to convert the lawyer's day into sellable chunks), and then the technology followed from this framework.

Viewed in this way, it strikes me that much of the recently developed law office technology does not have offsetting good-and-bad uses to which it might be put. For example, time-and-billing software is pretty well useless for legal clinics. High-tech "deal rooms" are worthless when representing immigrants seeking asylum or when practicing Constitutional law. There is no pressing need for a BlackBerry and a Web portal when handling simple divorces for working people. Upon closer inspection, most cutting-edge law office technology is oriented toward large firms that serve institutional clients on massive transactions with huge dollar figures. This technology does not serve clients *in general*; it serves a particular class of clients. Indeed, it is hard to see how any of this technology is particularly beneficial to a public interest lawyer; rather, it presumes the existence (and the legitimacy) of a profession in which the only goal is moneymaking and law is commoditized and sold by the hour. Even worse, the high cost of this technology is prohibitive for younger and more idealistic attorneys with neighborhood law practices, which has the pernicious result of skewing the technological playing field in favor of large firms, thereby undermining the adversary system and its presumption of relative equality between sides.

Despite all of our technological marvels, most people in America still cannot afford to hire a lawyer for any protracted legal problem. And despite all of the Web pages and Internet consultations offered by law firms, most Americans still cannot understand the law and have a profound distrust of lawyers. In fact, most Americans find themselves on the wrong end of the technology stick—forced to sign standard form contracts written by large firms, or on the receiving end of lawsuits and book-length discovery requests. Just as technology can devise atomic bombs without solving the problem of child poverty, it provides a small number of well-to-do law firms with superpowers while leaving the rest of the profession wholly unimproved.

For these reasons, young lawyers ought to be cynical about technology. To keep their values, young attorneys must set limits. After all, computer programs have no regulative capacity, the fax machine does not know when too much is too much, and the computer does not know how to shut itself off. Here is where we need to recall sociologist Lewis Mumford's prophetic warning in his groundbreaking treatise on technology: "The machine itself makes no demands and holds out no promises: it is the human spirit that makes demands and keeps promises."[33] Technology isn't *human*, so it has no sense of the *humane*, and it is indifferent to the uses to which it is put. The fax machine, e-mail, scanners, deal rooms, and other devices can run nonstop all day and all night. Alas, young lawyers cannot, and should not. One can be surrounded by machines without becoming a machine.

chapter seven:
Options for
Young Lawyers

In this book I have tried to account for a basic, incontrovertible fact: young lawyers are morosely unhappy. This is the verdict of countless surveys by bar associations and dozens of academic studies on young lawyers. Too many young lawyers find their lives alienating, their work demeaning, and their own behavior immoral. This is a terrible tragedy. The current system of legal education and practice is breeding a class of disaffected and cynical people who hate their profession.

There is no inherent reason why the legal profession should be so devastating. Law is a profession that should offer tremendous rewards and intellectual excitement. Law is a necessary part of any society that values freedom, democracy, due process, and social order. And lawyers are vitally necessary in a modern society governed by complicated laws that regulate every aspect of our lives, from citizenship to marriage, work, property, crime, business, and politics. We need smart and dedicated lawyers who love their work, who are willing to serve their clients without subverting justice, and who can earn a comfortable living without sacrificing their personal life. There is room in the legal profession for a diversity of interests, for corporate lawyers as well as public-interest lawyers, for maverick litigators and big-firm types, for giant law firms and solo practitioners. But a pluralistic, happy profession is possible only when young lawyers are free to shape their future from a range of options, as opposed to being thrown into a competitive sink-or-swim market after being saddled with crippling debts.

In order to discover what is wrong with the legal profession, I have painstakingly analyzed every step in the making of a young lawyer, in line with Ralph Nader's suggestion that "[a]nyone who wishes to understand the legal crises that envelop the contemporary scene—in the cities, in the environment, in the courts, in the marketplace, in public services, in the corporate-government arenas and in Washington—should come to grips with the flow chart that begins with the law schools and ends with the law firms, particularly the large corporate law firms of New York and Washington."[1] This is what I have tried to do in this book. I have traced the flow chart from law school to the big firms (as Nader suggests), and I have found a system that churns out amoral technocrats who are heavily in debt, desperate, easily manipulated, and dissociated from their own emotions and instincts. The legal profession now resembles a minefield stretching from law school to partnership, and even when a lawyer has made partner there is a constant specter of being "disequitized" (losing one's status as equity partner) for not attracting enough clients. If one makes it to the other end of this killing field, one looks around and thinks, "Could I have worked so hard for *this*?" They say that the worst experience is to get what one wants and to find it hollow. When I speak to my friends who finally make partner at prestigious law firms, or finally become lead counsel at top corporations, I am always surprised at their tentative demeanor and their inability to celebrate. They tell me that they feel like a contestant in a pie-eating contest for which first prize is a pie.

All young lawyers face a fundamental question of whether to stay in the profession or walk away. That is a question that you will have to answer for yourself, because I am not in the business of telling people how to live their lives. In my own case, I can only say that leaving the law was more difficult than I expected, in large part because my personal identity had become entwined with the profession. Although I felt that I was losing a piece of myself by staying in the profession, I also felt that an important part of myself was lost when I left the profession. In this chapter I would like to talk about the various factors that a young lawyer must weigh in deciding whether to stay in the profession or walk away, and I will suggest that for those of us who decide to stay, the best solution is to adopt a critical but hopeful posture toward the profession.

Reforming the Profession or Walking Away

A telling phenomenon occurs when a lawyer announces that she is leaving the practice of law: scores of other lawyers confess their hidden desire to do the same. This happened in my own case. On the day I left a large firm, I was besieged by phone calls and messages from disgruntled colleagues who came out of the woodwork to share their plans for leaving the profession. I have since come to realize that this is very common. I recently came across a similar story from a law professor who left a big firm for a low-paying academic job: "I was stunned two years ago when, after I announced that I was giving up my partnership in a big firm to teach, many of my colleagues and many other attorney friends told me how desperately they wanted to leave the practice of law. Almost without exception, they were successful lawyers who I thought were satisfied in their lives."[2] The same reaction was observed by author Walt Bachman, who left a long and distinguished practice in order to be a writer: "Time and again, lawyers at the pinnacle of their careers telephoned me or came into my office (usually closing the door discreetly behind them so as not to be overheard) to reveal their secret aspirations for escaping from their lives in the law. . . . Lawyers making up to a third of a million dollars a year expressed their vision of chucking it all to run a bait shop in northern Minnesota, teach inner-city kids, or manage a symphony orchestra."[3] These observations seem consistent with surveys of lawyers' unhappiness, and they suggest that unhappiness is not restricted to a few malcontents, but is a chronic and widespread condition among highly functioning lawyers. For every lawyer who actually leaves the profession, there are dozens who are repressing a similar urge.

Those who bail out of the profession have reached the conclusion that the problems of the profession are too deep-seated to be remedied. This is an understandable sentiment. If what I have said in this book is correct, we will need to change how young lawyers are educated, trained, licensed, apprenticed, and employed. Without question, every step of the current regime needs to be fundamentally changed. This task is daunting and overwhelming. The first task alone—reforming the law school curriculum—is a seemingly impossible project that could take decades. The struggle to reform the bar exam will require lawyers to speak out and expose themselves to retaliatory investigation by the bar authorities. And the struggle to change the structure and content of law firm practice could lead to banishment and financial ruin. To put the point cynically, there are lots of powerful people who benefit from the current regime that keeps young lawyers unhappy. We cannot expect them to casually disassemble a system that they have concocted to serve their own interests. At the same time, these are the people who throw around words like "ethics," "justice," and "freedom," so they are vulnerable to the accusation that they have created a system that fails by their own standards.

Unfortunately, there is no quick fix to the problem because there is no single enemy to blame for the predicament of young lawyers. The bottom line is that young lawyers have been made miserable by a number of disparate factors. The problems go back to the costs of law school, the pressures of the bar exam, the economic framework of law firms, the overcrowding of the profession, the technology that dominates legal practice, the increasing complexity of law, and so on. These factors meld together and conspire to generate a unified feeling of powerlessness and malaise, but there is no *single* enemy and no easy solution. We are not simply caught in a crisis of professionalism but in a crisis of law school, a crisis of the bar exam, a crisis of law firms, a crisis of ethics, a crisis of lawyer psychology, and so forth. This is a project requiring battle lines to be drawn on several fronts. We cannot blame everything on the decline of civility and professionalism, because these are mere symptoms of deeper problems. Indeed, there is something gratuitous and cruel when the so-called leaders of the bar (all of whom entered the profession when the climate was much easier) pontificate about how young lawyers are betraying the profession by abandoning the ideal of the lawyer-statesman. These admonishments are out of date and beside the point because they fail to come to terms with the massive pressures facing young lawyers, who do not have the luxury of being magnanimous Renaissance men. The problems facing young lawyers are *structural* and *economic*, which means that they cannot be solved by Miss Manners–style exhortations to behave well.

Of course, everyone wants a simple enemy to blame. There is a great scene in John Steinbeck's novel *The Grapes of Wrath* in which a farmer aims a gun at the henchmen who are trying to evict him, only to find out that they were hired by a bank, which is run by a board of directors, who are in turn run by a group of nameless and faceless financiers back East. Exasperated, the farmer complains, "But where does it stop? Who can we shoot?"[4] When the farmer declares his intention to visit the bank and explain his situation face-to-face, he is told, "It happens that every man in a bank hates what the bank does, and yet the bank does it. The bank is something more than men. Men made it, but they can't control it."[5] In a similar vein, some might argue that the legal profession has become a monster, something over and above the lawyers who made it, and that while every lawyer disagrees with the direction the profession is going, still the profession moves forward under its own inertia. This is actually what most lawyers believe—that the system is fatally flawed but impervious to change, so you might as well adapt to it.

But this is overly pessimistic. Older lawyers *constructed* this environment, and young lawyers can *deconstruct* it. The overpriced education that teaches so little, the ridiculous bar exam, the lack of quality jobs, the movement from a profession to a business—all of it is changeable.

The only way to create a better reality for young lawyers is to expose and cure the problems discussed in detail in this book. At the level of law school, students should demand instruction in basic lawyering skills, taught in a supportive environment by dedicated professors working closely with students. At the level of the bar exam, the challenge must come in the form of a protest that the exam is a form of gross overreaching by the state bar authorities, and that if the state is concerned that lawyers have basic competence, then they should adopt a system designed to provide competence without subjecting students to a bizarre ritual. At the level of practice, young lawyers must demand meaningful work, extensive client contact, and a reasonable lifestyle that balances professional challenges with personal time. All of this requires creative alternatives to the traditional law school, the traditional licensing scheme, the traditional law firm, and the factory model that presently dominates the practice of law. And it requires law students to stop obsessing over starting salaries and billable hours, and focus more on the *content* of what they should be doing.

There was never a Golden Age for the legal profession. But there was definitely a time when young lawyers had a wider range of choices and did not labor under such brutal constraints and restrictions. Lawyers of an older generation are now dying, and their autobiographies tell of a different era in the practice of law. Consider the case of Arthur Liman: he was a partner at the Paul, Weiss law firm in New York City, where he represented wealthy clients such as Pennzoil and Michael Milken, yet he also worked for the United States Attorney's Office, was involved in the state hearings on the Attica riots, counseled the Senate in the Iran-Contra hearings, and was president of the Legal Aid Society; his posthumous autobiography contains a foreword by the dean of Yale Law School.[6] Or consider the case of Arthur Kinoy, who started out as a union lawyer, was involved in trying to prevent the Rosenbergs' execution, was a leading lawyer in the Southern legal rights movement during the 1950s and 1960s, defended the Chicago Seven, founded the Center for Constitutional Rights, argued three cases before the

United States Supreme Court, and also taught as a professor at Rutgers School of Law.[7] It is hard to imagine a young lawyer nowadays following the example of these men and setting up a private practice, taking occasional public office, arguing cases before the Supreme Court, and teaching at the same time. But this freedom of movement is precisely the hallmark of a good profession. As Liman concluded, "To me, having a successful career in private life was more than earning a living. It gave me the independence when I took public assignments to do what I believed was right."[8] And yet by the time of his death in 1997, he was concerned that the profession had become obsessed with profits and money, converting lawyers into accountants.[9] Time will tell whether the legal profession as currently configured will turn out such well-rounded practitioners who can balance private practice with public commitment to justice.

Of course, the easiest path for the unhappy young lawyer is to simply walk away from the profession forever, although this is very rare because it requires abandonment of the considerable time and money that has already been invested. I can't blame anyone who walks away, because I did it myself after practicing law for five years. I look back with fondness on the day that I left the full-time practice of law. At the time, I thought it was my best day as a lawyer and the beginning of the rest of my life.

On an afternoon when all my colleagues were working hard preparing briefs and drafting contracts, I walked out of the law office and enrolled in graduate school to seek a doctorate in philosophy. While everyone else was fielding phone calls, writing down everything that they were doing as they were doing it, fretting over their time and the time spent fretting over their time, walking back and forth with a dull ache in the stomach and a thin layer of sweat from worrying about pleasing everyone above them—while all of this was happening, I was sitting in a coffee shop feeling a mixture of danger, foolishness, and emancipation. Somehow, in some way, I had thrown off the yoke of the law, silencing that disembodied voice that for years had told me I wasn't billing enough or wasn't deferent enough or as profitable as I should be. On that day, I raised my head and looked around, and I saw a very different world from the one that I had inhabited as a lawyer. The entire time that I was a practicing law I was so nervous and preoccupied and worried that I had never really stopped to look at the outside world—to simply look without judging.

What I saw after taking off my lawyers' glasses was a world where people could have direct relationships that weren't completely mediated by paperwork, where people spoke freely without fear and paranoia of being trapped in an inconsistent statement, where the clock was not a tyrant and where the day held promise of something good, something real, something that could affect the heart. There is an intoxication in leaving the strictures of the law, not merely for a vacation or a day off, but really leaving it for good and knowing that one will never again be a part of *that*. To leave the practice of law was tantamount to regaining my humanity, with all the fear, trouble, and promise that it brings, to have individual creativity, vulnerability, and a body of flesh, to actually live a life instead of documenting the lives of others. Put simply, I woke up as if from a nightmare and the world now had color, fluidity, dance, and shading. I had given up a safety net, it was true, but I had regained a part of myself that had been put on hold since college and was buried so deep that I had forgotten it.

That was a great day.

And yet, some years later, I found myself returning to the profession, as a law professor and part-time lawyer. Like so many others, I could not escape the law any more than I could escape any other part of myself. I was endlessly fascinated with legal controversies and with the way that the law veiled and legitimated power relations, and I loved to read and write about the law. Like it or not, I was a lawyer. And part of being a lawyer is to study how the law works, to speak out against injustice, to expose corrupt institutions, and to recommend positive reforms. So I came back to the law, this time with the goal of writing about the law and reforming it from within.

Most young lawyers have witnessed the destruction that I have documented in this book, yet they choose to remain in the profession, some out of hope, some because of fear, some out of ambition, some from inertia, and others because they love the idea of law as a helping profession, no matter how much that ideal suffers in the real world. Those of us who remain have the task of thinking critically about this profession and asking the tough questions that older lawyers are too afraid to handle. After all, we stand in a curious position. So many young people want desperately to join our ranks, while at the same time so many of our contemporaries search frantically for a way to leave. And in the end, those who simply bail out do nothing positive to improve the system.

Living with Yourself Morally and Psychologically

Those who remain in the profession generally adopt coping mechanisms to make life bearable. Psychologists sometimes speak of "fight-or-flight" as a natural human response to a threatening situation, but neither of these options is particularly attractive for young lawyers. *Fighting* can leave a young lawyer unemployed and vulnerable, while *flight* is tantamount to abandoning one's legal education and training. Instead of these options, unhappy lawyers tend to cope by either maintaining a rigid barrier between their personal and their professional identities, or merging their personal identity into their professional identity so that the two are inseparable. I call the first strategy *vertical split*[10] because it requires that the young lawyer split her authentic self from her role as a lawyer. I call the second strategy *colonization*[11] because the underlying personality is taken over by the professional identity.

Consider the case of a novice lawyer at a large firm who has the task of defending a powerful corporate executive against charges of sexual harassment. All of a sudden, the young lawyer finds herself filing dozens of motions to dismiss the lawsuit on the slightest pretext and filing onerous discovery requests, ultimately burying and outspending the plaintiff until the case is dropped. This young lawyer may believe strongly in corporate law and in the adversary system, which is fine, but her actions cut against everything that she has been taught about the justice system, due process, fairness, access to justice, and the adversary system as a method for discovering truth. This creates a conflict between her underlying personal values and the actions required in her role as a lawyer.

She is so disturbed by her situation that she divorces her *true-inner-layman-self* from a *false-outer-lawyer-self*, telling herself (and others) that "I am not what I do," or that "The law is just a job, but it isn't *me*," or "That's just my day job, I'm getting valuable experience." The problem with this, of course, is that it sets up a false barrier between two parts of a single person— you can be "yourself" for only a few hours a day, after work is over. A classic example of this split is a young lawyer who practices corporate law during the day but tries to be funky and alternative at night.

Another way to deal with this tension between oneself and one's professional role is to completely merge with the professional identity and blindly accept the rationalizations that buttress the existing state of the profession. In the example above, the lawyer might tell herself, "My role is to defend the client zealously, and that is what I have done, so I should be proud of myself." This, too, is a defense mechanism to ward off any qualms about one's behavior by depicting oneself as a player in a larger drama scripted by higher forces. But merging with one's role as a lawyer tends to eclipse the underlying person, which often leads to thinking and speaking in a legal capacity around the clock, to the point of adopting a cross-examining and paranoid style with one's spouse. In the worst-case scenario, the lawyer's internal sense of morality offers no check against her institutional role. This lawyer is never paralyzed with doubts about the profession, and this is precisely her problem: she *should* be embarrassed now and again by her actions as a lawyer (and by the profession generally), yet she never is.

The struggle with these extremes is common to all professions. The best-selling novel *The Remains of the Day* tells the story of a professional butler in England who swears absolute obedience to his master, even when this involves him in helping the master conspire with Nazis. In a wonderful passage, the butler describes the two coping mechanisms outlined above:

> And now let me posit this: "dignity" has to do crucially with a butler's ability not to abandon the professional being he inhabits. Lesser butlers will abandon their professional being for their private one at the least provocation. For such persons, being a butler is like playing some pantomime role; a slight push, a slight stumble, and the facade will drop off to reveal the actor underneath. The great butlers are great by virtue of their ability to inhabit their professional role and inhabit it to the utmost; they will not be shaken out of it by external events, however surprising, alarming, or vexing. They wear their professionalism as a decent gentleman will wear his suit: he will not let ruffians or circumstance tear it off him in the public gaze; he will discard it when, and only when, he wills to do so, and this will invariably be when he is entirely alone.[12]

Notice how this passage outlines two extreme positions—the professional who sees his role as a suit to be discarded versus the professional who lets the role colonize his personality, who never removes his suit. By sketching the alternatives so starkly he rules out a third, reasonable option: keeping some critical distance from your role. In my opinion, young lawyers must take this third option and learn to stand at a critical distance from their professional role, neither splitting off the role as totally artificial, nor merging with it completely.

A common defense mechanism for big-firm lawyers is to volunteer profusely for *pro bono* projects, to demonstrate to themselves and others that their values have not been compromised. Just as Penelope spun a web during the day and reversed her actions at night, *pro bono* is a valiant attempt to undo what a lawyer does on behalf of paying clients. But even if this fails, at least it shows some realization that the ordinary practice of law is so one-sided in favor of large institutions that it needs a counterweight. Lawyers who volunteer for *pro bono* should be praised because they recognize the existence of an underlying conflict and try to do something about it.

The truly scary young lawyers are the ones who fuse completely with their institutional role and view all others as weaklings who can't handle the demands of the profession. This perfectly described my mentor when I worked at the large firm. By all outward appearances he was successful, intelligent, hard working, professional, and happily married. He was everything that a recent law school graduate could ever hope to be. If rationality was measured by the ability to function within a large institution, he was immeasurably healthy. But after observing him for several years, I came to the opinion that he was insane, in a socially acceptable way.

This attorney proved amazingly adept at rationalizing anything that our clients wanted. Once we represented a Midwestern railroad that was warding off a hostile tender offer from a swashbuckling corporate raider from New York. In a heated meeting between the two sides, my mentor announced that the corporate raider had no business buying a railroad because he lacked an understanding of the history and legacy of the railroads. I was moved by his suggestion that there was something more at stake here than mere dollars and cents—we were talking about lives, vocations, and history. But two months later we represented a venture capital fund that was making a hostile bid for a pharmaceutical company. The lawyers for the drug company threw the same argument at us, claiming that our clients had no moral authority to take over a drug company since they lacked any training, interest, or understanding of the industry. My mentor replied, "It's a free country, anyone can buy anything." And just like that, he completely switched his position, without missing a beat.

A short while later we were reviewing documents drafted by the other side in a gigantic transaction. As usual, my mentor discovered some troubling language buried in a boilerplate provision drafted by the other side; the language could have been construed to impose personal liability on our clients.

"You see this shit," he complained to me. "That is dirty pool. That is why I come to work every morning, to find stuff like this to protect the clients. Don't forget, Litowitz, that we are in the business of protecting people."

Then I reminded him that we had just spent a month drafting similar documents full of the same little tricks in favor of our own clients, virtually identical to the dirty tricks we were denouncing from the other side.

"Doesn't it seem a little hypocritical to think of ourselves as *protectors*, when we are also *attackers*?" I mused.

He was irate. "We don't attack anybody, we merely protect our clients." Through this sleight of hand, he exonerated himself from the very conduct that he found so objectionable in other lawyers.

Routinely, this attorney would have me draft corporate documents that contained unfair provisions binding on the corporation's employees and customers. Whenever I pointed out that such provisions were grossly unfair and probably unenforceable, he would say, "Welcome to America." By this statement, he ridiculed my concerns as naive, completely inverting basic morality: *He* was not to blame for drafting illegal and immoral provisions, but instead *I* was to blame for blowing the whistle. I had to keep reminding myself: A person who says anything and tramples on weak people for money is a spineless hypocrite, regardless of whether he is wearing an expensive suit.

There is a longstanding mistake among lawyers that the underlying *person* cannot be blamed for what his *role* requires him to do. In other words, all responsibility "falls on the role,"[13] as it were, leaving the person blameless. This view was described nicely by French philosopher Michel de Montaigne: "An honest man is not accountable for the vice or stupidity of his trade, and should not therefore refuse to practice it: it is the custom of his country, and there is profit in it. We must live in the world and make the most of it such as we find it."[14] In other words, whether the role of corporate lawyer is played by Doug Litowitz or some other hopeful young lawyer, the role of corporate lawyer will be played by someone, so it might as well be me.

This is the attitude of most lawyers. And it is nonsense. Roles do not play themselves—they require actors. And if enough people refuse a role, then it will eventually change. And if the entire system is such that people are so desperate that they will play any role (no matter how despicable) in order to make a buck, then the entire system is corrupt. As things stand, most of the unethical, immoral, stultifying, obfuscatory, delaying, and harassing conduct by lawyers is rationalized as fidelity to their role as a zealous advocate in an adversary system. But these lawyers are simply cowards who are looking for an excuse, too afraid to sit down and think about the real human tragedies that they are perpetuating through their roles. The burdens of life are not lifted by counting oneself a cog in a wheel, especially when the wheel itself is a system that perpetuates and justifies inequality.

The healthy lawyer recognizes the need for maintaining a professional demeanor and following the rules of professional conduct, while simultaneously holding tenaciously to her fundamental sense of justice as a counterweight that can challenge, limit, and restrain the role she is playing. The key is to accept role-playing as a necessary aspect of professional service, but to understand that the role is itself answerable to larger moral considerations. The healthy lawyer follows the rules of the profession, but not blindly, and sometimes not at all. She retains sufficient autonomy to reject some of her clients' projects as immoral or wasteful, and she has critical distance to recognize that her profession and the legal system in general are deeply flawed. This requires a delicate balance and constant negotiation so that she can internalize certain aspects of her professional identity without completely abandoning herself to an uncritical fusion with her role.

The difficult trick is to remain proud of your profession while also being a little bit ashamed of it.

Notes

Chapter One

1. Ann Hagedorn, "Lawyers Have High Rate of Mental Health Woes," *Wall Street Journal*, November 30, 1990, B1; David Margolick, "More Lawyers Are Less Happy at Their Work, a Survey Finds," *New York Times*, August 17, 1990, B5; Deborah Arron, *Running from the Law* (1989; reprint, Seattle: Niche Press, 2004).

2. American Bar Association, *At the Breaking Point: The Report of a National Conference on the Emerging Crisis in the Quality of Lawyers' Health and Lives, and Its Impact on Law Firms and Client Services* (Chicago: American Bar Association, 1991).

3. Seth Rosner, "A Decade of Professionalism," *Professional Lawyer* 9 (August 1995): 2.

4. Amy Stevens, "Why Lawyers Are Depressed, Anxious, Bored Insomniacs," *Wall Street Journal*, June 12, 1995, B1.

5. Dick Dahl, "The Trouble with Lawyers," *Boston Globe Magazine*, April 14, 1996, 26; Maura Dolan, "Miserable with the Legal Life; More and More Lawyers Hate Their Jobs, Survey Finds," *Los Angeles Times*, June 27, 1995, A1.

6. Sol Linowitz (with Martin Mayer), *The Betrayed Profession* (New York: Scribner, 1994); Walt Bachman, *Law v. Life: What Lawyers Are Afraid to Say about the Legal Profession* (New York: Four Directions, 1995); Anthony Kronman, *The Lost Lawyer: Failing Ideals of the Legal Profession* (Cambridge: Harvard University Press, 1993).

7. Sandra Day O'Connor, *The Majesty of the Law: Reflections of a Supreme Court Justice* (New York: Random House, 2003), 225.

8. W. Dale Nelson, "O'Connor: Lawyers 'Unhappy Lot': First Woman Justice Visits University of Wyoming," *Casper (Wyoming) Star-Tribune*, March 17, 2004, 1.

9. Stephen Breyer, "The Legal Profession and Public Service," a speech at the Pierre Hotel in New York City, September 12, 2000, sponsored by the National Legal Center for the Public Interest, available at http://www.supremecourtus.gov/publicinfo/speeches/speeches.html.

10. Edward Re, "The Causes of Popular Dissatisfaction with the Legal Profession," *St. John's Law Review* 68 (1994): 85, 87–95; American Bar Association, *Public Perception of Lawyers: Consumer Research Findings* (Chicago: American Bar Association, April 2002) (only 19 percent of consumers expressed confidence in lawyers, as opposed to 50 percent for doctors). The growing unpopularity of lawyers is discussed by Leonard Gross, "The Public Hates Lawyers: Why Should We Care?" *Seton Hall Law Review* 29 (1999): 1405, 1416 ("A 1993 survey showed a worsening of the images of lawyers since 1986. . . . The public's opinion of lawyers had declined still further by 1996").

11. Andrew Benjamin, Elaine Darling, and Bruce Sales, "The Prevalence of Depression, Alcoholism, and Cocaine Abuse among United States Lawyers," *International Journal of Law and Psychiatry* 13 (1990): 233. For a discussion of this data, see Larry Krieger, "Healthy, Happy, and Sane: The Road to Professionalism," *Florida State University Law Magazine*, Winter 1998, 9–10.

12. Benjamin et al., "The Prevalence of Depression," 234; Stevens, "Why Lawyers Are Depressed," B1 (citing a Johns Hopkins study finding that lawyers were more likely to be depressed than members of 104 other professions, while a study from Campbell University found that 11 percent of North Carolina lawyers contemplated suicide at least once a month).

13. Connie Beck, Bruce Sales, and Andrew Benjamin, "Lawyer Distress: Alcohol-Related Problems and Other Psychological Concerns among a Sampling of Practicing Lawyers," *Journal of Law and Health* 10 (1995): 1, 49.

14. Kelly Pedone, "Shifting Gears," *Texas Lawyer*, April 19, 2004 (reporting that nearly 30 percent of Texas law grads are pursuing nonlegal jobs, and that a survey by the American Bar Association found that 65 percent of attorneys would consider switching jobs within the next two years); "Stress Outweighs Pay as Lawyers Flee Profession," *Chicago Tribune*, March 11, 1990, C1 (American Bar Association survey finds that lawyers are reporting increasing stress, alcohol consumption, and dissatisfaction). The late 1980s and early 1990s saw the emergence of books aimed at lawyers who sought to leave the profession, such as Mary Ann Altman, *Life After Law* (Washington, DC: Wayne Smith, 1991); Mark Byers, Don Samuelson, and Gordon Williamson, *Lawyers in Transition* (Natick, Mass.: Barkley, 1988).

15. Daphne Eviatar, "Out of Court: Evidence Shows Lawyers Are Leaving the Legal Profession," *Christian Science Monitor*, April 17, 2000, 11. For a discussion of lawyers thinking about leaving the profession, see Jill Chanen, "Lawyers Finding Satisfaction in Getting Out or Scaling Down," *Chicago Lawyer,* March 1994, 4; Nancy Holt, "Are Longer Hours Here to Stay?" *American Bar Association Journal*, February 1993, 62.

16. John Sebert, "The Cost and Financing of Legal Education." *ABA Syllabus* 35 (February 2004): 1, 5 (noting that 80 percent of students borrow money to finance their legal education, while aggregate indebtedness for these students was $84,400. Actual law school debt—not including undergraduate—averaged $44,592 for students at public law schools and $68,805 for students at private schools).

17. These figures are from the National Association for Law Placement, as reported by Joseph Harbaugh, "Legal Education Economics 101: A Primer for Bar Examiners," *Bar Examiner*, November 2001, 21, n. 14.

18. Ed Finkel, "Banks and Law Schools Offer Grads Tips on Scaling Mt. Debt," *Chicago Lawyer*, April 1994, 70.

19. Josh Richmond, "Fellow Alumni Speak Up for Law Grad Hounded by Feds," *Oakland Tribune*, September 24, 2004, 2004 WL 94449298.

20. See the Web page maintained by the National Association of Public Interest Lawyers, http://www.napil.org: "The meteoric rise in law school tuition has resulted in astronomical law student debt, currently averaging $80,000." The NAPIL encourages law students to enter public interest positions through a loan deferment program.

21. Equal Justice Works, National Association for Law Placement, and Partnership for Public Service, *From Paper Chase to Money Chase: Law School Debt Diverts the Road to Public Service* (2002), 22, available at http://www.equaljusticeworks.org.

22. Eric Herman, "Law Graduates of 1994 Find Field of Delayed Dreams in Job Searches," *Chicago Lawyer*, July 1994, 4.

23. Barbara Curran, *Women in the Law: A Look at the Numbers* (Chicago: American Bar Association, 1995), 7.

24. Harbaugh, "Legal Education Economics 101." Starting salaries for private firms and public interest jobs are collected by the National Association for Law Placement, and are available on their Web site at http://www.nalp.org.

25. Gary Hengstler, "Vox Populi: The Public Perception of Lawyers: The ABA Poll," *American Bar Association Journal*, September 1993, 60.

26. Martin Garbus and Joel Seligman, "Sanctions and Disbarment: They Sit in Judgment," in Ralph Nader and Mark Green, eds., *Verdicts on Lawyers* (New York: Thomas Crowell, 1976), 47.

27. Stuart Rothenberg, "Lawyers, Politicians, and Other Hypocrites in Florida's

Presidential Race," Cable News Network, November 27, 2000, available at http://archives.cnn.com/2000/allpolitics/stories/11/27/rothenberg.column.

28. Kathy Sawyer, "Statistics: When the Numbers Are Victim," *Washington Post*, June 19, 1995, A2.

29. "Dershowitz Redux (Letters)," *Nation*, December 15, 2003, 2 (letter of Alan Dershowitz regarding instructions to research assistant and research staff to check original documents).

30. Greg Morago, "Where Are They Now? Key Players in Simpson Case," *Orlando Sentinel*, June 13, 2004, F3.

31. Alison Frankel, "Civil Inaction," *American Lawyer*, March 2002, 82 (chronicling the difficulty of poor African Americans in finding a lawyer to represent them in a toxic tort case against polluters in the Florida panhandle, even after the Environmental Protection Agency was convinced that the pollution had caused personal injuries).

32. "Offshore: Framing Cayman," *Lawyer*, March 29, 2004, 49 (referring to *New York Times* article noting that Enron had 881 Caribbean subsidiaries); David Evans, "Corporations Flock to Tax Havens," *Orlando Sentinel*, June 27, 2004, H4 (claiming that Enron had 441 subsidiaries in the Cayman Islands alone).

33. Jim Yardley and John Schwartz, "Enron's Collapse: The Law Firm: Legal Counsel in Many Ways Mirror Clients," *New York Times*, January 16, 2002, C6.

34. *Lincoln Savings & Loan v. Wall*, 743 F. Supp. 901, 919–20 (D. D.C. 1990) (Sporkin, J.).

35. Robert A. Ferguson, *Law and Letters in American Culture* (Cambridge: Harvard University Press, 1984), 11.

36. Kronman, *The Lost Lawyer*.

37. Linowitz, *The Betrayed Profession*.

38. Timothy Terrell and James Wildman, "Rethinking 'Professionalism,'" *Emory Law Journal* 41 (Spring 1999): 403, 424.

39. Rob Atkinson, "A Dissenter's Commentary on the Professionalism Crusade," *Texas Law Review* 74 (1995): 259.

40. Robert Kurson, "Who's Killing the Great Lawyers of Harvard?" *Esquire Magazine*, August 2000, 82.

41. Michael Trotter, *Profit and the Practice of Law: What's Happened to the Legal Profession* (Athens: University of Georgia Press, 1997), 32 (estimating that he billed 1,400 hours in an Atlanta law firm in the mid-1960s).

42. Scott Turow, "Law School vs. Reality," *New York Times*, September 18, 1988, section 6, 52, 71–72.

43. Kurson, "Who's Killing?"

44. William Keates, *Proceed with Caution* (Chicago: Harcourt Brace Legal & Professional Publishing, 1997), 142.

45. Kara Scannell, "Revenues Increase 9.5% at Top U.S. Law Firms," *Wall Street Journal*, June 29, 2004, C3 ("America's richest law firms got even richer last year and a lot of that wealth lined the pockets of equity partners").

46. George Orwell, *Coming Up for Air* (New York: Harvest Books, 1983).

47. Amiram Elwork and Andrew Benjamin, "Lawyers in Distress," *Journal of Psychiatry & Law* 23 (Summer 1995): 205, 209.

48. Susan Diacoff, "Asking Leopards to Change Their Spots: Should Lawyers Change? A Critique of Solutions to Problems with Professionalism by Reference to Empirically-Derived Attorney Personality Attributes," *Georgetown Journal of Legal Ethics*

11 (1998): 547 (suggesting that lawyers have certain personality characteristics that cannot be altered by changes to the environment of legal practice).

49. Carl Horn III, *LawyerLife: Finding a Life and a Higher Calling in the Practice of Law* (Chicago: American Bar Association, 2003) (contains a concise summary of the empirical studies on lawyer unhappiness).

50. William Eaton, J. C. Anthony, W. Mandel, and R. Garrison, "Occupations and the Prevalence of Major Depressive Disorder," *Journal of Occupational Medicine* 32 (1990): 1079. Mike Snider, "Even Lawyers Get the Blues," *USA Today*, November 27, 1990, 1A (discussing the Johns Hopkins study).

51. Daphne Eviatar, "Out of Court"; Judith Schroer, "Running from the Law: Discontented Lawyers Flee Profession," *USA Today*, October 7, 1993, B1; Deborah Hensler and Maria Reddy, *California Lawyers View the Future: A Report to the Commission on the Future of the Legal Profession and the State Bar* (Santa Monica, CA: RAND, 1994).

52. Marci Alboher Nusbaum, "Private Sector: Closing His Eyes, He Sees a Path," *New York Times*, September 28, 2003, Money & Business section, 2 ("Each year, legions of lawyers flee the profession").

53. Snider, "Even Lawyers Get the Blues" ("Lawyers are 3.6 times more likely to suffer depression than people in other fields, recent findings show"); A. J. Flick, "O'Connor to Lawyers: Restore Dignity to Field," *Tucson Citizen*, June 15, 2004, A3 (Justice O'Connor stated that lawyers are three times more likely than the general population to suffer from depression, suicide, divorce, and drug abuse).

54. Diacoff, "Asking Leopards to Change Their Spots," 555–57 (discussing studies on law students compared to students from other professional schools).

55. Karl Marx and Friedrich Engels, *Manifesto of the Communist Party* (New York: Washington Square, 1976), 69.

56. Derrick Nunnally, "State's Law Students Get a Free Pass on Bar Exam: Despite Detractors, Age-Old Privilege Likely to Remain," *Milwaukee Journal Sentinel*, August 7, 2004, B1.

57. Lawrence Friedman, *A History of American Law* (New York: Simon & Schuster, 1973), 652.

58. Herbert Marcuse, *One-Dimensional Man* (Boston: Beacon, 1964), 226.

59. Roland Barthes, *Mythologies* (New York: Hill & Wang, 1972), 11.

60. Soren Kierkegaard, *Concluding Unscientific Postscript to Philosophical Fragments* (Princeton: Princeton University Press, 1992), 167.

Chapter Two

1. Andrew Benjamin, Elaine Darling, and Bruce Sales, "The Prevalence of Depression, Alcohol Abuse, and Cocaine Abuse among United States Lawyers," *International Journal of Law and Psychiatry* 13 (1990): 233.

2. Susan Diacoff, "Asking Leopards to Change Their Spots: Should Lawyers Change? A Critique of Solutions to Problems with Professionalism by Reference to Empirically-Derived Attorney Personality Attributes," *Georgetown Journal of Legal Ethics* 11 (1998): 547, 556 (discussing the various studies).

3. Marilyn Heins, S. Fahey, and L. Heiden, "Perceived Stress in Medical, Law and Graduate Students," *Journal of Medical Education* 59 (1984): 205; Marilyn Heins, Shirley Fahey, and Roger Henderson, "Law Students and Medical Students: A

Comparison of Perceived Stress," *Journal of Legal Education* 33 (1983): 511; Connie Beck, Bruce Sales, and Andrew Benjamin, "Lawyer Distress: Alcohol-Related Problems and Other Psychological Concerns among a Sampling of Practicing Lawyers," *Journal of Law and Health* 10 (1995): 1, 4 (although medical students showed elevated psychological problems, their levels did not match those of law students).

4. Gerry Spence, *The Making of a Country Lawyer* (New York: St. Martin's, 1996), 245.

5. *The Paper Chase* (Twentieth Century Fox, 1973).

6. Scott Turow, *One L* (New York: Warner Books, 1977), 25.

7. Michael Carney, "Narcissistic Concerns in the Education Experience of Law Students," *Journal of Psychiatry & Law*, 18 (Spring-Summer 1990), 9, 33 n. 24.

8. Harvard Law School Association, *Report of the Ninth Annual Meeting* (orig. 1895), reprinted in Bernard Schwartz, ed., *Main Currents of American Legal Thought* (Durham, NC: Carolina Academic Press, 1993), 348.

9. Charles Warren, *History of Harvard Law School and Early Legal Conditions in America*, vol. 2 (New York: Lewis, 1908), 374.

10. Ibid., 361, 374.

11. Scott Turow, "Law School vs. Reality," *New York Times*, September 18, 1988, section 6, at 52, 71.

12. Jerome Frank, *Courts on Trial: Myth and Reality in American Justice* (Princeton: Princeton University Press, 1950), 225.

13. Alan Dershowitz, *The Best Defense* (New York: Vintage, 1983), 17.

14. Pierre Schlag, "Normativity and the Politics of Form," *University of Pennsylvania Law Review* 139 (1991): 801.

15. Robert Kurson, "Who's Killing the Great Lawyers of Harvard?" *Esquire Magazine*, August 2000, 82.

16. Richard Kahlenberg, *Broken Contract: A Memoir of Harvard Law School* (New York: Hill and Wang, 1999), 5.

17. Tom Stabile, "Debt Help on the Way," *Pre-Law Insider*, Spring 2002, 21.

18. These figures come from the National Association of Public Interest Lawyers (NAPIL), as quoted in Stabile, "Debt Help on the Way."

19. Joseph Harbaugh, "Legal Education Economics 101: A Primer for Bar Examiners," *Bar Examiner*, November 2001, 26.

20. Hakim Bey, *T.A.Z.: The Temporary Autonomous Zone, Ontological Anarchy, Poetic Terrorism* (Brooklyn, NY: Autonomedia, 1991), 114.

21. Leo Tolstoy, *The Death of Ivan Illych* (New York: Bantam, 1981), 126–27.

22. Marion T. D. Lewis, *The Law School Rules* (New York: Harmony Books, 2000), 23.

23. Duncan Kennedy, "Legal Education as Training for Hierarchy," in David Kairys, ed., *The Politics of Law* (New York: Pantheon Books, 1990), 38.

24. Roger Schechter, "Changing Law Schools to Make Less Nasty Lawyers," *Georgetown Journal of Legal Ethics* 10 (1996): 367, 393.

25. "Law Students Tackle Criminal Code Grounded in Islamic Law," Associated Press Wire, available at http://www.cnn.com/2004/EDUCATION/10/08/penn.islamic. law.ap/index.html; Gordon Smith and Cynthia Williams, *Business Organizations: Cases, Problems and Case Studies* (New York: Aspen, 2004).

Chapter Three

1. American Bar Association Commission on Professionalism, *In the Spirit of Public Service: A Blueprint for Rekindling of Lawyer Professionalism* (Chicago: American Bar Association, 1986), reprinted at 112 F.R.D. 243, 261–62 (1986).

2. Christiana Sciaudone, "This Test-Taker Raised the Bar for Perseverance," *Los Angeles Times*, May 21, 2004, B2. Governor Pataki recently appointed an official to head the Public Service Commission after failing the New York bar seven times. Wayne Barrett, "New York's Price of Darkness," *Village Voice*, August 26, 2003, 20.

3. Hilary Clinton, *Living History* (New York: Simon & Schuster, 2003), 64 (she passed in Arkansas and failed in D.C.); Gerry Spence, *The Making of a Country Lawyer* (New York: St. Martin's, 1996), 263.

4. Lawrence Friedman, *A History of American Law* (New York: Simon & Schuster, 1973), 652.

5. Albert Woldman, *Lawyer Lincoln* (New York: Carroll & Graf, 1994), 164–65.

6. Magali Larson, *The Rise of Professionalism: A Sociological Analysis* (Berkeley: University of California Press, 1977), 173.

7. Thomas Morgan and Ronald Rotunda, *Professional Responsibility: Problems and Materials* (Westbury, NY: Foundation, 1991), 48, 61 (citing statistics showing that neglect and overreaching are the primary reasons for clients to file a complaint with the bar authorities).

8. "New York State Bar Association Releases 1998 Lawyer Discipline Figures," *State Bar News*, New York State Bar Association, September/October 1999. In 1999, only 242 lawyers out of 112,000 were disciplined. See "Discipline Report Shows Drop in Complaints against Lawyers," *State Bar News*, September/October 2000.

9. Fyodor Dostoevsky, "A Disgraceful Affair," in *Great Short Works* (New York: Harper Collins, 1968), 249.

10. Shirley Jackson, *The Lottery and Other Stories* (New York: Noonday, 1992).

11. Barbara Ehrenreich, *Nickeled and Dimed: On (Not) Getting By in America* (New York: Metropolitan Books, 2001), 59.

12. Karl Marx, *The 18th Brumaire of Louis Bonaparte*, in Robert Tucker, ed., *The Marx-Engels Reader* (New York: Norton, 1978), 598.

13. BAR/BRI Digest, *National Bar Exam Information* (Richard J. Convisor, Publisher, 2005 edition), 36 (advertisement for New York Essay Advantage).

14. Marcia Kuechenmeister, "Admission to the Bar: We've Come a Long Way," *Bar Examiner*, February 1999, 25 (discussing the evolution of the MBE and MPT).

15. See "2003 Statistics," *Bar Examiner*, May 2004, 23.

16. Deborah Merritt, Lowell Hargens, and Barbara Reskin, "Raising the Bar: A Social Science Critique of Recent Increases to Passing Scores on the Bar Exam," *University of Cincinnati Law Review* 69 (2001): 929, 939.

17. Terence L. Blackburn, "Make Bar Exams Relevant," *Broward Daily Business Review*, October 25, 2004, 6 ("the real issue facing Florida and other states is whether bar examinations themselves are an adequate measure of attorney competence.")

18. John Caher, "New York Raising Bar Exam Passing Grade," *New York Law Journal*, September 27, 2004, 1.

19. Deborah Jones Merritt, "Raising the Bar: Limiting Entry to the Legal Profession," *Bar Examiner*, November 2001, 10.

20. Laurie Cunningham, "Raising the Bar: In Decision Split over Methodology and

Goals, State Supreme Court Raises the Bar Exam Pass Level," *Broward Daily Business Review*, March 26, 2003, A1 (noting that the previous scaled score of 131 required getting 56 percent of the questions correct).

21. The statistics are gathered annually and published by the National Conference of Bar Examiners. The numbers cited here are from "2003 Statistics," *Bar Examiner*, May 2004, 6.

22. Derrick Nunnally, "State's Law Students Get Free Pass on Bar Exam," *Milwaukee Journal Sentinel*, August 6, 2004, B1.

23. Maurice Possley, "Law Firm's Rising Star Trapped in a Lie after 10 Years," *Chicago Tribune*, May 6, 1988, A1.

24. Friedrich Engels, letter to Franz Mehrings (July 14, 1898), quoted in Christopher Pines, *Ideology and False Consciousness* (Albany: State University of New York Press, 1993), 1.

25. *Application of Griffiths*, 413 U.S. 717, 93 S. Ct. 2851 (1973).

26. *Supreme Court of New Hampshire v. Piper*, 470 U.S. 274, 105 S. Ct. 1272 (1985).

27. Morgan and Rotunda, *Professional Responsibility*, 37–40, citing *Konigsberg v. State Bar*, 353 U.S. 252, 77 S. Ct. 722 (1957).

28. *Birbrower, Mentelbano, Condon, & Frank v. Superior Court of Santa Clara County*, 949 P.2d 1 (Calif. 1998).

29. Anthony Davis, "Multijurisdictional Practice by Transactional Lawyers: Why the Sky Really Is Falling," *Bar Examiner*, February 2001, 15.

30. Jennifer Binkley, "Admission on Motion: Current Practices and Rules," *Bar Examiner*, November 2000, 22.

31. Daniel Minnich, George Riemer, and Robert Welden, "Reciprocal Admission between Idaho, Oregon, and Washington," *Bar Examiner*, February 2002, 21.

32. The statistics are kept by the Florida Bar and displayed on the Florida Bar's comprehensive Web page under the title "Selected Disciplinary Statistics," http://www.flabar.org.

33. Deborah Rhode, "Moral Character as a Professional Credential," *Yale Law Journal* 94 (1985): 491, 591.

34. Wade Lambert, "Bar Debates Screening Out Mentally Ill," *Wall Street Journal*, March 10, 1995, B1.

35. Tim O'Brien, "Cuba Trips, Cigars Sink Bar Applicant," *New Jersey Law Journal*, September 8, 2003, 1.

36. Thomas Adcock, "Pilot Proposal Would Make Public Service Count on New York Bar Exam," *New York Law Journal*, June 28, 2002, 16.

37. Victoria Rivkin, "Bye Bye Bar Exam?: New York Program Would Offer Some Grads Alternative to the Written Test," *American Bar Association Journal*, February 2003, 16; Thomas Adcock, "Groups Decry Increase in Bar Exam Cut Score," *New York Law Journal*, October 1, 2004, 1.

Chapter Four

1. American Bar Association Commission on Professionalism, *In the Spirit of Public Service: A Blueprint for Rekindling Lawyer Professionalism* (Chicago: American Bar Association, 1986), reprinted at 112 F.R.D. 243 (1986); Diane Molvig, "The Economics

of Practicing Law: A 2001 Snapshot," *Wisconsin Lawyer*, December 2001, 6 (estimating that overhead per lawyer is $68,654).

2. William Keates, *Proceed with Caution* (Chicago: Harcourt Brace Legal and Professional Publications, 1997), 142.

3. Marx predicted: "As a rule, the whole guild system declines and falls, both master and journeyman, where the capitalist and the worker arise." *The Grudrisse*, in Robert Tucker, ed., *The Marx-Engels Reader* (New York: Norton, 1978), 270.

4. Karl Marx and Friedrich Engels, *Manifesto of the Communist Party*, in *The Marx-Engels Reader*, 476 (emphasis added).

5. Illinois Rules of the Supreme Court, Article VIII, Preamble to the Illinois Rules of Professional Conduct, effective August 1, 1990.

6. Roger Parloff, "Skadden: A Flexible Firm Breaks the Billion Dollar Barrier," *American Lawyer*, July 2000, 88.

7. Roger Parloff, "Overbilled by $57 Million?" *American Lawyer*, May 1994, 65.

8. One of the attorneys for Reynolds apparently gave a speech in April of 1988 in which he boasted, "To paraphrase General Patton, the way we won these cases was not by spending all of Reynolds' money, but by making the other son of a bitch spend all of his." Quoted in Ralph Nader and Wesley Smith, *No Contest: Corporate Lawyers and the Perversion of Justice in America* (New York: Random House, 1996), 27.

9. Marx's theory of alienation is set forth most fully in his early essay, "Estranged Labor," in *The Economic and Philosophical Manuscripts of 1844*, reprinted in *The Marx-Engels Reader*, 66.

10. Gerry Spence, *With Justice for None* (New York: Times Books, 1989), 64.

11. Edward Re, "The Causes of Popular Dissatisfaction with the Legal Profession," *St. John's Law Review* 68 (1994): 85, 95.

12. Marx and Engels, *Manifesto*, 474: "Society as a whole is more and more splitting up into two great hostile camps facing each other: Bourgeoisie and Proletariat."

13. I am following the definition of bourgeoisie and proletariat given by Engels in the *Manifesto*: "By 'bourgeoisie' is meant the class of modern capitalists, owners of the means of social production and employers of wage labor. By 'proletariat,' the class of modern wage laborers who, having no means of production of their own, are reduced to selling their labor power in order to live." (*Manifesto*, 473).

14. Nancy Holt, "Are Longer Hours Here to Stay?" *American Bar Association Journal*, February 1993, 65.

15. Robert Kurson, "Who's Killing the Great Lawyers of Harvard?" *Esquire Magazine*, August 2000, 82.

16. Michael Trotter, *Profit and the Practice of Law* (Athens: University of Georgia Press, 1997), 32.

17. Cameron Stracher, "Show Me the Misery," *Wall Street Journal*, March 6, 2000, A31.

18. William Rehnquist, "The Legal Profession Today," *Indiana Law Journal* 62 (1987): 151, 154, 155.

19. *Bates v. State Bar of Arizona*, 433 U.S. 350, 97 S. Ct. 2691 (1977) (permitting lawyer advertising); *Goldfarb v. Virginia State Bar*, 421 U.S. 773, 95 S. Ct. 2004 (1975) (striking minimum fee schedules).

20. Trotter, *Profit and the Practice of Law*, 29.

21. "Billing Alternatives Offered," *National Law Journal*, December 18, 2000, B15.

22. Jim Dunlap, "Billable Hours Under Attack," *American Bar Association Journal*, March 2002, 23.

23. Russell Pearce, "The Professional Paradigm Shift: Why Discarding Professional Ideology Will Improve the Conduct and Reputation of the Bar," *New York University Law Review* 70 (1995): 1229.

24. William Glaberson, "Megafirms Are Taking Over Corporate Law," *Business Week*, November 17, 1986, 104.

25. Alison Frankel, "Veil of Tiers," *American Lawyer*, July 2004, 92.

26. Ibid.

27. Marie Beaudette, "Associates Giving Up on Partnership," *Legal Times*, September 29, 2004, 1.

28. Amanda Ripley, "A Shock to the System," *Legal Times*, June 26, 2000, 45.

29. Susan Hansen, "The Young and the Restless," *American Lawyer*, September 1995, 66.

30. Deborah Rhode, *In the Interests of Justice* (New York: Oxford University Press, 2000), 5.

31. "Bar Talk: Of Money and Misery," *American Lawyer*, April 1999, 31.

32. Darlene Ricker, "Greed, Ignorance, and Overbilling," *American Bar Association Journal*, August 1994, 65.

33. "Skaddenomics," *American Lawyer*, September 1991, 3.

34. Tom Herman, "Ernst & Young will Finance Launch of Law Firm in Special Arrangement," *Wall Street Journal*, November 3, 1999, B10.

35. Bill Quinn, *How Wal-Mart Is Destroying America* (Berkeley, CA: Ten Speed Press 2000).

36. Anthony Lin, "Big Law Contract Attorneys Struggle with Their Identity as 'Lawyers,'" *New York Law Journal*, October 18, 2004, 1.

37. Marx, "Estranged Labor," in *The Marx-Engels Reader*, 70.

38. Ibid., 71–72.

39. Marx, "Wage Labor and Capital," in *The Marx-Engels Reader*, 204.

40. Marx, "Estranged Labor," 74.

41. Holt, "Are Longer Hours Here to Stay?"

42. Maura Dolan, "Miserable with the Legal Life," *Los Angeles Times*, June 27, 1995, A1.

43. Marx, "Estranged Labor," 76.

44. Marc Galanter, "Big Tobacco: Winning by Losing," *American Lawyer*, January/February 1999, 55.

45. Rone Tempest, "Enron Counsel Warned about Partnerships," *Los Angeles Times*, January 31, 2002, Business Section, 1.

46. Marx, "Estranged Labor," 77.

47. Marx, "The Meaning of Human Requirements," in *The Marx-Engels Reader*, 147.

48. Karl Marx, *Capital*, vol. 3 (New York: Vintage Books, 1981), 969.

49. Karl Marx, *Capital*, vol. 1 (New York: Vintage Books, 1977), 899.

50. Marc Galanter and Thomas Palay, *Tournament of Lawyers: The Transformation of the Big Law Firm* (Chicago: University of Chicago Press, 1991), 28.

51. Arron, *Running from the Law*; Daphne Eviatar, "Out of Court: Evidence Shows Lawyers Are Leaving the Legal Profession," *Christian Science Monitor*, April 17, 2000, 11.

52. "Following the Money?" *New York Law Journal*, June 25, 2004, 16 (noting an average public interest starting salary of $49,000 and an average debt load of $100,000);

National Association for Law Placement, *2004 Survey, Public Sector and Public Interest Attorney Salary Report*, http://www.nalp.org/press/pi_sal04.htm.

53. The most coherent discussion of mentoring, along with a proposal for a mentoring program, can be found in Walter Bennett, *The Lawyer's Myth: Reviving Ideals in the Legal Profession* (Chicago: University of Chicago Press, 2001).

54. Alex Keller, "Professionalism: Where Has It Gone?" *Colorado Lawyer* 14 (1985): 1383, 1385.

55. Pearce, "The Professional Paradigm Shift," 1251–52.

Chapter Five

1. Anthony Kronman, *The Lost Lawyer* (Cambridge: Harvard University Press, 1993), 273.

2. Amy Mashburn, "Professionalism as a Class Ideology: Civility Codes and Bar Hierarchy," *Valparaiso Law Review* 28 (1994): 657.

3. John Heinz et al., *The Scale of Justice: Observations on the Transformation of Urban Law Practice* (Chicago: American Bar Foundation Working Paper, May 2000).

4. Richard Abel, *American Lawyers* (New York: Oxford University Press, 1989), 183.

5. Emily Barker, "Winston & Strawn Gets Ruthless," *American Lawyer*, June 1993, 70.

6. John Grisham, *The Firm* (New York: Island Books, 1992), 68.

7. Lisa Lerman, "Lying to Clients," *University of Pennsylvania Law Review* 138 (1990): 659, 759.

8. Quoted in Ralph Nader and Wesley Smith, *No Contest: Corporate Lawyers and the Perversion of Justice in America* (New York: Random House, 1996), 27.

9. Mark Dombroff, "Winning Is Everything," *National Law Journal*, September 25, 1989, 13.

10. Mashburn, "Professionalism as a Class Ideology," 658.

11. Rachel Katz, "Ex-Kmart CEO to Get at Least $9.5 Million," *Chicago Sun-Times*, March 19, 2002, 63.

12. David Leonhardt, "Watch It: If You Cheat, They'll Throw Money," *New York Times*, June 8, 2002, section 3, pg. 1.

13. Nicholas Kristof, "Millions for Moochers," *New York Times*, March 6, 2004, A15.

14. *Circuit City v. Adams*, 279 F.3d 889 (9th Cir. 2002).

15. David Johnston, "Enron Avoided Income Taxes in 4 of 5 Years," *New York Times*, January 17, 2002, A1.

16. *Circuit City v. Adams*.

17. Model Rule of Professional Conduct 2.1, adopted by over forty states, specifically says that, "a lawyer may refer not only to law but to other considerations, such as moral, economic, social and political factors that may be relevant to the client's situation."

18. Sanson's life is discussed at length in Arthur Isak Applbaum, *Ethics for Adversaries* (Princeton: Princeton University Press, 1999), 20.

19. Andrew Ross Sorkin, "Tyco Defense Begins Closing Argument," *New York Times*, March 16, 2004, C6.

20. Quoted in Sigmund Freud, *Group Psychology and the Analysis of the Ego* (New York: W. W. Norton, 1959), 6.

21. "Adolph Eichmann in His Own Words," from *The Trial of Adolph Eichmann*, PBS Special, at www.pbs.org/eichmann/ownwords.htm.

22. Hannah Arendt, *Eichmann in Jerusalem: A Report on the Banality of Evil* (New York: Penguin Books, 1994).

23. Christopher Browning, *Fateful Months: Essays on the Emergence of the Final Solution* (New York: Holmes & Meier, 1985), 64–65.

24. Robert Merton, *Social Theory and Social Structure* (New York: Free Press, 1968), 252–53.

25. Stanley Milgram, *Obedience to Authority: An Experimental View* (London: Tavistock, 1974).

26. David Luban, *Lawyers and Justice* (Princeton: Princeton University Press, 1988), xx.

27. *Walters v. Nat'l Assoc. Radiation Survivors*, 473 U.S. 305, 105 S. Ct. 3180, 3190 (1985).

28. Judge Frank Easterbrook, quoted in Sanford Levinson, "Frivolous Cases: Do Lawyers Really Know Anything at All?" *Osgoode Hall Law Journal* 24 (1987): 353, 375.

29. Arthur Levitt, *Take on the Street* (New York: Pantheon, 2003), 44.

30. 148 *Congressional Record* S6554, S6556 (July 10, 2002) (statements of Senator Michael Enzi and Senator Jon Corzine).

31. Paul Braverman, "Helter Shelter," *American Lawyer*, November 2003, 65, 68.

32. "Day in the Life: Corporate Law Associate," posted on Vault.com, Law School Section, September 1, 2001.

33. M. A. Stapleton, "Pitfalls of Practicing Law Outlined by Author," *Chicago Daily Law Bulletin*, January 31, 1997, 3.

34. "Bar Talk: Of Money and Misery," *American Lawyer*, April 1999, 31.

Chapter Six

1. John Stuart Mill, *Principles of Political Economy*, quoted in Karl Marx, *Capital*, vol. 1 (New York: Vintage Books, 1977), 492.

2. Mark Voorhees, "Faraway Pay Day: When Will Firms' Investment in Technology Produce Dividends?" *American Lawyer Technology Supplement*, March 2000, 23.

3. Sigmund Freud, *Civilization and Its Discontents* (New York: W. W. Norton, 1961), 38–39.

4. Thorstein Veblen, *The Instinct of Workmanship* (New York: Huebsch, 1922).

5. Joann Lublin, "Vacation Is Anything But for a Chief Executive at Play," *Wall Street Journal*, July 23, 1997, B1.

6. Alex Markels, "Memo 4/8/97, FYI: Messages Inundate Offices," *Wall Street Journal*, April 8, 1997, B1.

7. Ibid.

8. Sue Shellebarger, "Overwork, Low Morale Vex the Mobile Office," *Wall Street Journal*, August 17, 1994, B1.

9. Anita Dennis, "A Firm without Walls," *Journal of Accountancy*, December 1995, 62–63.

10. Ibid.

11. Douglas Stewart, "The Office To Go," *Inc. Magazine Office Advisor*, Fall 1992, 27.

12. Joe Cappo, "Paper Blizzard Buries 'Office of the Future,' " *Crain's Chicago Business*, April 17, 1989, 6.

13. Jim Calloway, "Scanners: One of Today's Most Indispensable Pieces of Law Office Equipment," *Oklahoma Bar Journal*, January 1998, 237.

14. Guido Calabresi, *A Common Law for the Age of Statutes* (Cambridge: Harvard University Press, 1982) (chapter 1, "Choking on Statutes").

15. Corinne Cooper, ed., *The New Article 9, Uniform Commercial Code* (Chicago: American Bar Association Section on Business Law, 2000).

16. H.L.A. Hart, *The Concept of Law* (New York: Oxford University Press, 1994), 117.

17. Philip Howard, *The Death of Common Sense* (New York: Warner Books, 1996), 49.

18. Peter Goodrich, *Legal Discourses* (New York: St. Martin's, 1987), 7.

19. Franz Kafka, "The Problem of Our Laws," in *The Complete Stories* (New York: Schocken Books, 1971), 437–38.

20. Terry Carter, "A Justice Who Makes Time to Read, and Thinks All Lawyers Should, Too," *Chicago Daily Law Bulletin*, January 26, 1993, 2.

21. Bayless Manning, "Hyperlexis and the Law of Conservation of Ambiguity: Thoughts on Section 385," *Tax Lawyer* 36 (1982): 9.

22. Ibid., 13.

23. Jorge Luis Borges, "The Library of Babel," in *Labyrinths* (New York: W. W. Norton, 1988), 51.

24. Adam Liptak, "Stop the Clock? Critics Call the Billable Hour a Legal Fiction," *New York Times*, October 29, 2002, G7.

25. Brad Malamud, "How Times Have Changed: A Systematic Approach to Billing," *Defense Counsel Journal* 62 (October 1995): 583.

26. Lewis Mumford, "The Mechanical Routine," in Eric and Mary Josephson, eds., *Man Alone: Alienation in Modern Society* (New York: Dell, 1962), 114–17.

27. Jean Baudrillard, "Consumer Society," in *Jean Baudrillard: Selected Writings* (Stanford: Stanford University Press, 1988), 29–30.

28. Richard Roeper, "Reality Check Due for Cyber-Geek Gates," *Chicago Sun-Times*, November 30, 1995, 11.

29. Bill Gates, *The Road Ahead* (New York: Viking, 1995), 4.

30. David Bilinsky, *Amicus Attorney in One Hour for Lawyers* (Chicago: American Bar Association Law Practice Management Section, 2000), vi.

31. Karl Jaspers, *The Origin and Goal of History* (New Haven: Yale University Press, 1953), 115.

32. Martin Heidegger, *The Question concerning Technology* (New York: Garland, 1977), 12. ("Technology is no mere means. Technology is a way of revealing.")

33. Lewis Mumford, *Technics and Civilization* (New York: Harcourt, Brace, 1934), 6.

Chapter Seven

1. Ralph Nader, "Law Schools and Law Firms," *New Republic*, October 11, 1969, 20.

2. Patrick Schiltz, "Legal Ethics in Decline: The Elite Law Firm, the Elite Law School, and the Moral Formation of the Novice Attorney," *Minnesota Law Review* 82 (1998): 705.

3. Walt Bachman, *Law v. Life: What Lawyers Are Afraid to Say about the Legal Profession* (New York: Four Directions, 1995), 12.

4. John Steinbeck, *The Grapes of Wrath* (New York: Viking, 1989), 52.

5. Ibid., 45.

6. Arthur Liman, *Lawyer: A Life of Counsel and Controversy* (New York: Public Affairs, 1998).

7. Arthur Kinoy, *Rights on Trial: The Odyssey of a People's Lawyer* (Cambridge: Harvard University Press, 1983).

8. Clyde Haberman, "Arthur L. Liman, a Masterly Lawyer, Dies at 64," *New York Times*, July 18, 1997, A23.

9. Liman, *Lawyer*, 362 (afterword by Judith Resnik).

10. Arnold Goldberg, *The Problem of Perversion* (New Haven: Yale University Press, 1995), 14.

11. The reference here is to Jurgen Habermas's notion of the colonization of the life-world by the instrumental rationality and strategic communication in the economic and administrative contexts. Jurgen Habermas, *The Theory of Communicative Action*, vol. 2 (Cambridge: Polity, 1987), 353.

12. Kazuo Ishiguro, *The Remains of the Day* (New York: Vintage, 1989), 42–43. The implications of this novel for lawyers are discussed by Rob Atkinson, "How the Butler Was Made to Do It: The Perverted Professionalism of *The Remains of the Day*," *Yale Law Journal* 105 (1995): 177.

13. This notion comes from David Luban, *Lawyers and Justice* (Princeton: Princeton University Press, 1988), 117.

14. Michel de Montaigne, "Of Husbanding Your Will," in Donald Frame, ed., *The Complete Essays of Montaigne* (Stanford: Stanford University Press, 1958), 773.

Index